A Handbook of
Structured
Experiences
for
Human
Relations
Training

Volume VIII

Edited by

J. WILLIAM PFEIFFER, Ph.D.

JOHN E. JONES, Ph.D.

UNIVERSITY ASSOCIATES
Publishers and Consultants
8517 Production Avenue
P. O. Box 26240
San Diego, California 92126

SERIES IN HUMAN RELATIONS TRAINING

PREFACE

In the two years since the appearance of Volume VII of this series, we have received a great number of structured experiences from users of the *Handbooks*. This current volume represents our selection of the most widely useful of these designs. We remain interested in receiving writeups of structured experiences for possible inclusion in future issues and in our companion publication, *The Annual Handbook for Group Facilitators*.

This volume, like most of its predecessors, contains two dozen structured experiences, most of them original. Users are encouraged to adapt and modify them to suit their own unique needs and circumstances. In producing this volume, we have tried to make the designs as generally applicable as possible, avoiding those suited only to relatively specialized uses.

As with all University Associates publications, users may freely reproduce these materials for educational or training purposes. *For large-scale distribution or the inclusion of materials in publications for sale, prior written permission is required.*

We at University Associates continue to hold the professional value that resources should be shared by peers. The *Handbooks of Structured Experiences for Human Relations Training* are one important evidence of this belief. We continue to invite users to participate in this process, through feedback suggestions and by sending us materials that have proven helpful to them.

We are very grateful to many people who have helped make this volume of the *Handbook* possible, among them Phyliss Cooke and Tim Nolan, who served as content consultants, and Arlette Ballew, staff editor, whose endless patience with details deserves a special note of recognition.

J. William Pfeiffer
John E. Jones

San Diego, California
December, 1980

TABLE OF CONTENTS

*See Introduction, p. 3, for explanation of numbering.

INTRODUCTION

Our early work in creating learning designs led us to the use of what had always been termed "exercises," "techniques," or "games." When we made the decision to gather these valuable materials into a book, we became concerned that "exercise" and "game" had connotations we considered dysfunctional to the intent of their use. We therefore elected to call them "structured experiences," to indicate that they are designed for experience-based learning.

Our interest in providing participants with a distinctive design for human relations training has resulted in an increasing orientation in our consulting activities, laboratories, and workshops toward experiences that produce generally predictable outcomes. In designing human relations training experiences, we strive to become aware of and to examine the specific needs of the client system or particular group and then develop learning situations that will meet those needs. Based on an experiential model, structured experiences are inductive rather than deductive, providing *direct* rather than vicarious learnings. Thus, participants *discover* meaning for themselves and *validate* their own experience.

A variety of experiential learning models have been developed in recent years (see Palmer, 1981). Our own version has five steps that occur in a cycle:

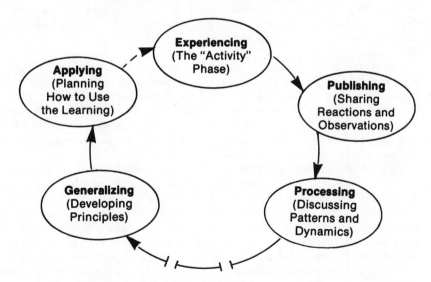

The *experiencing* phase involves some activity such as fantasy, dyadic sharing, or group problem solving. If the model stopped at this point, however, training would be only "fun and games." Next, the participants engage in *publishing* their reactions to and observations of the activity. This is the data-generation phase; it leads logically into *processing*. It is our belief that processing is the key to the potency of structured experiences, and it is important that the facilitator allow sufficient time for this step. If the training is to transfer to the "real world," it is important for the participants to be able to extrapolate the experience from a laboratory setting to the outside world through *generalizing*. In this phase, participants develop principles, hypotheses, and generalizations that can be discussed in the final phase, *applying*. This final phase must not be left to chance; facilitators need to ensure that participants recognize the relevance of the learning. The actual application of behavior becomes a new experience and begins the cycle again.

There is no successful way to cut short this cycle. If structured experiences are to be effective, the facilitator must supply adequate opportunities for "talk-through." The payoff comes when the participants learn *useful* things that they take responsibility for applying.

Thus, a concern that we bring to all our training publications is the need for adequate processing of the training experience so that participants are able to integrate the learning without the stress generated by unresolved feelings about the experience. It is at this point that the expertise of the facilitator becomes crucial if the experience is to be responsive to the learning and emotional needs of the participants. The facilitator must judge whether he or she will be able successfully to process the data that probably will emerge in the group through the structured experience. Any facilitator, regardless of background, who is committed to the growth of individuals in the group can usefully employ structured experiences. The choice of a particular activity must be made using two criteria: the facilitator's competence and the participants' needs.

As in the previous volumes of the *Handbook*, the sequencing of structured experiences in Volume VIII has been based on the amount of understanding, skill, and experience needed by the facilitator to use each experience effectively. The first structured experience, therefore, requires much less background on the part of the facilitator than does the last. The earlier experiences generate less affect and less data than do those near the end of the book, and, consequently, the facilitator needs less skill in processing to use them effectively and responsibly.

It is also the responsibility of the facilitator to examine the specific needs and the level of sophistication of the group and to choose a suitable structured experience. Adaptability and flexibility are therefore emphasized in the design of the structured experiences in this volume. The variations listed after each structured experience suggest possible alterations that a facilitator may wish to incorporate in order to make the experience more suitable to the particular design and to the needs of the participants. The expected norm in human relations training is innovation.

Our use of and experimentation with structured experiences led us to an interest in developing useful, uncomplicated questionnaires, opinionnaires, and other instruments. It is our belief that instruments enhance and reinforce the learning from structured experiences. Instruments also provide feedback to the facilitator on the appropriateness of the activity and the effectiveness of the presentation.

Some instruments appeared in the first volumes of these *Handbooks* and have subsequently been revised and refined in later editions. Each volume of the *Handbooks* contains structured experiences that include instruments. We find that the complementary selection of structured experiences and instruments can create powerful learning environments for participants, and we encourage those involved in the field of human relations training to become acquainted with this twofold approach in providing for participants' learning needs.

At the end of each structured experience in this volume are cross references to similar structured experiences, suggested instruments, and lecturette sources that seem especially appropriate to that experience. The number of each supplemental or complementary structured experience and the publication in which it appears are indicated. Instruments and lecturettes are listed by title and publication. Space for notes on each structured experience has been provided for the convenience of the facilitator.

Our published structured experiences are numbered consecutively throughout the series of *Handbooks* and *Annuals*, in order of publication of the volumes. A list of all structured experiences from all volumes of the *Handbook* and all volumes of the *Annual*. One feature of the *Kit* is that each structured experience has been rated according to (a) how much affect is likely to be generated, (b) how structurally complex the design is, and (c) how difficult the activity is to process.

The contents of the entire series of *Handbooks* and *Annuals* are fully indexed in the revised *Reference Guide to Handbooks and Annuals*. The *Reference Guide* is an indispensable aid in locating a particular structured experience or a structured experience for a particular purpose, as well as related instruments, lecturettes, and theory articles.

The purpose, then, of the *Handbooks* is to share further the training materials that we have found to be useful in training designs. Some of the experiences that appear here originated within University Associates, and some were submitted to us by facilitators in the field. It is gratifying to find that facilitators around the world are using the *Handbooks* and concur with our philosophy that sharing these valuable materials with others is far more in the spirit of human relations theory than the stagnating concept of "ownership" of ideas.

Users are encouraged to submit structured experiences, instruments they have developed, and papers they have written that might be of interest to practitioners in human relations training. In this manner, our Series in Human Relations Training will continue to serve as a clearinghouse for ideas developed by group facilitators.

REFERENCE

Palmer, A. Learning cycles: Models of behavioral change. In J. E. Jones & J. W. Pfeiffer (Eds.), *The 1981 annual handbook for group facilitators*. San Diego, CA: University Associates, 1981.

293. NAME TAGS: AN ICE BREAKER

Goals

    I. To provide participants with an opportunity to introduce themselves in a nonthreatening and enjoyable manner.

    II. To develop an atmosphere conducive to group interaction.

Group Size

    A minimum of eight participants.

Time Required

    Fifteen minutes.

Materials

    I. A name tag for each participant.

    II. A pencil for each participant.

Physical Setting

    A room with a cleared space to accommodate group movement.

Process

    I. The facilitator introduces the activity as an ice breaker and gives each participant a name tag and a pencil. He instructs the participants to fill out their name tags and wear them.

    II. The facilitator directs the participants to introduce themselves to someone in the group whom they do not know. He says that both persons are then to exchange information about themselves for two minutes.

    III. When time is called, the facilitator directs each participant to exchange name tags with the person he is talking to and then go on to meet *another* participant and discuss *only* the person whose name tag he is wearing. (Two minutes.)

    IV. When the facilitator calls time, the participants switch name tags again and find others to talk to, talking only about the persons whose name tags they are wearing, as before.

V. The facilitator continues this process for as many rounds as necessary for the size of the group, so that most of the participants have met.

VI. The facilitator tells each participant to retrieve his own name tag.

VII. Participants debrief the activity by making a brief statement to the total group about who they are, as in round one. Participants may also share reactions and awarenesses about the introduction experience.

Similar Structured Experiences: *Vol. I:* Structured Experience 5; *Vol. II:* **42**; *Vol. III:* **49**; *'73 Annual:* **87, 88**; *Vol. IV:* **101**; *'74 Annual:* **125**; *76 Annual:* **174**.

Suggested Instruments: *'74 Annual:* "Interpersonal Communication Inventory," "Self-Disclosure Questionnaire."

Notes on the Use of "Name Tags":

Submitted by Don Martin and Cynthia Cherrey.

294. LEARNING EXCHANGE: A GETTING-ACQUAINTED ACTIVITY

Goals

I. To provide an opportunity for participants to get to know each other.

II. To demonstrate the knowledge and skills that the participants have brought to the group.

III. To raise awareness of factors that enhance the teaching-learning process.

Group Size

Any number of dyads.

Time Required

Approximately one hour.

Materials

I. A blank 3″ x 5″ index card for each participant.

II. A pencil for each participant.

III. Newsprint and felt-tipped markers.

Physical Setting

A room large enough that each dyad can work without disturbing the others.

Process

I. The facilitator introduces the goals of the activity. He states that much of what we learn has little to do with schools or teachers but, rather, occurs as people seek to pursue their hobbies or to solve life's daily problems. He cites as examples learning how to repair a faucet, make chili con carne, take out a second mortgage, mix cement, or plan a political campaign.

II. The facilitator encourages the participants to recall some of the skills they have acquired in this informal way during the past year and to select one or two of these skills that they could teach to another person.

III. The facilitator distributes blank index cards and pencils to the participants and says that participants are to write their names and the skills they are prepared to teach on the cards.

IV. The facilitator collects the skill cards, lays them out in the middle of the room, and directs the participants to examine all the cards and *either* select a skill they would like to learn *or* agree to teach their skill to another participant. (Five minutes.)

V. The pairs of participants, each consisting of a teacher and a learner, then engage in the teaching-learning process. (Ten minutes.)

VI. The selection and teaching-learning process is repeated with different pairs of participants. (Ten minutes.)

VII. The entire group reconvenes, and participants report briefly on their experiences during the teaching-learning sessions. (Ten minutes.)

VIII. The facilitator lists on newsprint the factors that seem to enhance teaching and learning as these are identified by the participants and then leads a brief discussion of how these learnings can be used. (Ten minutes.)

Variations

I. The participants can list learning needs rather than skills. These learning needs can then be reviewed by all the participants in order to identify those members who can teach the desired skills.

II. The activity can be conducted only once.

III. In debriefing the activity, the facilitator can use the principles for effective learning and teaching that are agreed on by the participants to establish categories for a feedback sheet to monitor subsequent progress of the learning group.

Similar Structured Experiences: *Vol. II:* Structured Experience **26**; *'73 Annual:* **91.**

Suggested Instruments: *'74 Annual:* "S-C (Student-Content) Teaching Inventory"; *'79 Annual:* "Training Style Inventory (TSI)."

Submitted by Andy F. Farquharson.

Notes on the Use of "Learning Exchange":

295. PEOPLE ON THE JOB: EXPRESSING OPINIONS

Goals

I. To afford participants the opportunity to share their views in a structured environment.

II. To provide a sense of the variety of opinions and attitudes that exist about a particular subject.

III. To develop a climate for future group interaction.

Group Size

Any number of groups of five to seven members each.

Time Required

One and one-half to two hours.

Materials

I. A copy of the People on the Job Work Sheet for each participant.

II. A pencil for each participant.

III. Newsprint and a felt-tipped marker.

Physical Setting

A room in which each group can be seated in a circle.

Process

I. The facilitator briefly reviews the goals of the activity.

II. The facilitator gives a copy of the People on the Job Work Sheet and a pencil to each participant. Participants are instructed to take no more than fifteen minutes to respond to the twenty statements.

III. The facilitator calls time and divides the participants into groups of five to seven members each. The members of each group are instructed to discuss the statements and their responses. The members are also told that they may change any of the responses on their People on the Job Work Sheets as a result of the discussions within their groups. (Twenty-five minutes.)

IV. The total group is reassembled, and the members share their reactions to the experience. The following points can be posed to the group members for their comments:

1. On which items was there a significant difference of opinion?
2. Did the group's discussion cause any members to change their opinions?
3. Did members defend their own opinions? Did members try to convince others to change their opinions?

(Twenty minutes.)

V. The facilitator forms new subgroups to process the experience. Group members are directed to discuss their personal learnings and to consider the implications of these learnings for themselves and for managers in their roles as supervisors. (Fifteen to twenty minutes.)

VI. The facilitator calls for a reporter from each group to share a key learning from the group about people on the job. (Fifteen minutes.)

VII. Generalizations and applications are then drawn from these subgroup learnings. (Fifteen minutes.)

Variations

I. A shorter or modified version of the People on the Job Work Sheet can be used.

II. Between step II and step III, the facilitator can instruct members to "line up" on a continuum to indicate their responses to selected items from the work sheet.

III. The participants can select a few items of particular interest to group members to discuss during step III, e.g., items on which they are in agreement/disagreement, items representing the widest range of opinion, etc.

Similar Structured Experiences: *Vol. I:* Structured Experience **24**; *'73 Annual:* **94**; *'79 Annual:* **244**; *Vol. VIII:* **304**.

Suggested Instruments: *'72 Annual:* "Supervisory Attitudes: The X-Y Scale"; *'75 Annual:* "Diagnosing Organization Ideology"; *'80 Annual:* "Increasing Employee Self-Control (IESC)."

Lecturette Sources: *'72 Annual:* "Assumptions About the Nature of Man," "McGregor's Theory X-Theory Y Model"; *'75 Annual:* "The Supervisor as Counselor"; *'76 Annual:* "Making Judgments Descriptive"; *'79 Annual:* "Anybody with Eyes Can See the Facts!"

Submitted by Martin B. Ross.

Notes on the Use of "People on the Job":

PEOPLE ON THE JOB WORK SHEET[1]

1. It is only human nature for people to do as little work as they can get away with.

   Agree .... *Undecided* .... *Disagree*

2. If employees have access to any information they want, they tend to have better attitudes and behave more responsibly.

   Agree .... *Undecided* .... *Disagree*

3. One problem in asking for the ideas of employees is that their perspective is too limited for their suggestions to be of much practical value.

   Agree .... *Undecided* .... *Disagree*

4. If people do not use much imagination and ingenuity on the job, it is probably because relatively few people have much of either.

   Agree .... *Undecided* .... *Disagree*

5. People tend to raise their standards if they are accountable for their own behavior and for correcting their own mistakes.

   Agree .... *Undecided* .... *Disagree*

6. It is better to give employees both the good and the bad news because most people want the whole story, no matter how painful it is.

   Agree .... *Undecided* .... *Disagree*

7. Because a supervisor is entitled to more respect than those below him in the organization, it weakens his prestige to admit that a subordinate was right and he was wrong.

   Agree .... *Undecided* .... *Disagree*

8. If you give people enough money, they are less likely to be concerned with such intangibles as responsibility and recognition.

   Agree .... *Undecided* .... *Disagree*

9. If people are allowed to set their own goals and standards of performance, they tend to set them higher than management would.

   Agree .... *Undecided* .... *Disagree*

---

[1]Adapted from *Every Employee a Manager* by M. Scott Myers. Copyright ©1970, McGraw-Hill. Used with permission of McGraw-Hill Book Company.

10. The more knowledge and freedom a person has regarding his job, the more controls are needed to keep him in line.

    Agree .... *Undecided* .... *Disagree*

11. When people avoid work, it is usually because their work has been deprived of its meaning.

    Agree .... *Undecided* .... *Disagree*

12. If employees have access to more information than they need to do their immediate tasks, they will usually misuse it.

    Agree .... *Undecided* .... *Disagree*

13. Asking employees for their ideas broadens their perspectives and results in the development of useful suggestions.

    Agree .... *Undecided* .... *Disagree*

14. Most people are imaginative and creative but may not show it because of limitations imposed by supervision and the job.

    Agree .... *Undecided* .... *Disagree*

15. People tend to lower their standards if they are not punished for their misbehavior and mistakes.

    Agree .... *Undecided* .... *Disagree*

16. It is better to withhold unfavorable news about business because most employees really want to hear only the good news.

    Agree .... *Undecided* .... *Disagree*

17. Because people at all levels are entitled to equal respect, a supervisor's prestige is increased when he supports this principle by admitting that a subordinate was right and he was wrong.

    Agree .... *Undecided* .... *Disagree*

18. If you give people interesting and challenging work, they are less likely to complain about such things as pay and supplemental benefits.

    Agree .... *Undecided* .... *Disagree*

19. If people are allowed to set their own goals and standards of performance, they tend to set them lower than management would.

    Agree .... *Undecided* .... *Disagree*

20. The more knowledge and freedom a person has regarding his job, the fewer controls are needed to ensure satisfactory job performance.

    Agree .... *Undecided* .... *Disagree*

296. BOSS WANTED: IDENTIFYING LEADERSHIP CHARACTERISTICS

Goals

    I. To allow individuals to examine their personal criteria for a good manager.

    II. To compare preferences about managerial qualities.

    III. To increase awareness of one's own current managerial strengths and weaknesses.

Group Size

    Ten to fifteen participants.

Time Required

    Approximately one and one-half hours.

Materials

    I. Five sample newspaper advertisements for managerial positions appropriate to the group.

    II. Blank paper and a pencil for each participant.

    III. Newsprint and a felt-tipped marker.

Physical Setting

    A room large enough to allow the groups to meet separately, preferably around tables.

Process

    I. The facilitator discusses the goals of the activity. (Five minutes.)

    II. The facilitator reads aloud the "want ads" for managers or displays them with an overhead projector. (The advertisements should be for managerial positions that relate to the occupations of the participants.)

    III. Blank paper and pencils are distributed to the participants.

IV. The participants are directed to form groups according to which advertisement they are most attracted to. Each group is given a copy of its chosen ad to refer to during the activity.

V. The groups are directed to expand and clarify their advertisements, listing both the "essential" and "desirable" characteristics they believe the applicant must have. (Fifteen minutes.)

VI. Each group presents its list of required and desired attributes, and members of other groups request clarification and respond. (Fifteen minutes.)

VII. Subgroups meet again, and members individually evaluate themselves in terms of their group's criteria. Group members then discuss their self-evaluations and offer each other suggestions for improvements. (Twenty minutes.)

VIII. The entire group assembles to discuss the experience. The following sequence is followed to debrief and process the activity:
1. Members' reactions to differing managerial criteria.
2. Summary reports on subgroup discussions.
3. New learnings about self.
4. New learnings about managerial characteristics or requirements.
5. Ways in which members plan to apply new insights in their back-home work situations.

(Twenty minutes.)

Variations

I. When working with intact groups or groups in which participants are known to each other, the subgroup members can be instructed to share perceptions of their managerial strengths and solicit feedback from other group members during step VII.

II. One list can be developed during step VI to represent the thinking of all the subgroups. Members then evaluate their strengths and weaknesses based on this list.

III. Subgroups can be formed and given the task of identifying managerial criteria common to all five of the want ads. Personal strengths and weaknesses are then the focus of the discussion.

IV. Subgroup members can write "job wanted" ads for themselves, focusing on their managerial strengths. These are shared in the subgroups or read aloud to the large group.

Similar Structured Experience: '74 *Annual:* Structured Experience **127**.

Suggested Instruments: '73 *Annual:* "LEAD (Leadership: Employee-Orientation and Differentiation) Questionnaire"; '75 *Annual:* "Diagnosing Organization Ideology"; '81 *Annual:* "Patterns of Effective Supervisory Behavior."

Lecturette Sources: '74 *Annual:* "The 'Shouldist' Manager"; '75 *Annual:* "Participatory Management: A New Morality"; '76 *Annual:* "Leadership as Persuasion and Adaptation"; '79 *Annual:* "The Centered Boss."

Notes on the Use of "Boss Wanted":

Based on material submitted by Graham L. Williams.

297. GROUP EFFECTIVENESS: A TEAM-BUILDING ACTIVITY

Goals

I. To increase team members' understanding of the concept of group effectiveness.

II. To generate commitment within an intact group to identify its interaction dynamics.

Group Size

Five to twelve members of an ongoing (or intact) group.

Time Required

Approximately two hours.

Materials

I. Blank paper and a pencil for each participant.

II. Newsprint and felt-tipped markers for each group.

III. Masking tape.

Physical Setting

A room large enough for subgroups to meet without disturbing each other and with wall space for posting newsprint.

Process

I. The facilitator discusses the goals of the activity and gives an overview of the design. (Five minutes.)

II. Paper and pencils are distributed, and individuals are instructed to brainstorm a list of "what makes a group of people effective in accomplishing its objectives." (Five minutes.)

III. A recorder is appointed to make a "round-robin" listing of these dimensions on newsprint. (Ten minutes.)

IV. The facilitator instructs the group to reduce this list to its essential components—not more than six dimensions. Some suggested procedures are:

1. Vote for three
2. Rank-order the top ten
3. Categorize the basic list.

(Fifteen minutes.)

V. The members are directed to create a model or graphic representation of how the dimensions are related to each other. (Twenty minutes.)

VI. The facilitator forms subgroups. Each subgroup creates on newsprint a behaviorally anchored rating scale (BARS)[1] for one or more dimension(s) assigned to the group by the facilitator. The facilitator may display the following example on newsprint:

Participation

1	2	3	4	5	6	7	8	9

There is unevenness of participation in the group's deliberations; members hold back a lot.

All group members participate about equally and attentively in group interactions; members freely volunteer inputs.

(Twenty minutes.)

VII. Each subgroup presents its BARS chart(s) to the entire group; the charts are edited by the entire group for clarity. (Twenty minutes.)

VIII. The facilitator instructs individuals to respond to each of the rating scales according to how the group *usually* works together (before this session). The members are then instructed to rate the effectiveness of the group during this work session. (Five minutes.)

IX. The facilitator leads the group in developing a "progress" chart of its effectiveness and in plotting its two sets of ratings obtained so far. (Ten minutes.)

X. The facilitator leads a discussion of the data obtained in the ratings. The group may decide to continue using its instrument to chart its development in the future. (Ten minutes.)

XI. The facilitator draws out learnings from the activity and directs attention to how the team can manage its own effectiveness. (Fifteen minutes.)

Variations

I. The team can write prescriptions for improving its effectiveness.

---

[1]For a brief discussion of behaviorally anchored rating scales, see the Introduction to the Instrumentation Section in the 1980 *Annual*.

II. The entire activity can be carried out in a larger group, with subgroups organized to survey all members on their BARS individually.

III. In a larger group, subgroups can complete step VII and then apply their models to another group rather than to themselves. Subgroups can then prepare feedback reports for each other.

Similar Structured Experiences: *Vol. I:* Structured Experience **10**; *Vol. III:* **55, 66**; *'72 Annual:* **79**; *'73 Annual:* **92.**

Suggested Instruments: '74 *Annual:* "Reactions to Group Situations Test"; '76 *Annual:* "Organization Behavior Describer Survey."

Lecturette Sources: '72 *Annual:* "Guidelines for Group Member Behavior"; '80 *Annual:* "Interaction Process Analysis."

Notes on the Use of "Group Effectiveness":

Submitted by John E. Jones and Anthony J. Reilly.

298. LIFELINE: A VALUE-CLARIFICATION ACTIVITY

Goals

I. To increase awareness of social influences on the formation of attitudes, beliefs, values, and perceptions.

II. To examine personal development and growth in the context of political history, social movements, and popular culture.

III. To share differing values and orientations.

Group Size

Several groups of four to six members each.

Time Required

One and one-half hours.

Materials

I. A copy of the Lifeline Work Sheet for each participant.

II. A pencil for each participant.

III. Newsprint and a felt-tipped marker.

Physical Setting

A room large enough to allow the groups to work without interfering with each other.

Process

I. The facilitator explains the goals of the activity and provides a brief orientation to the topic of the importance of social influences on the formation of values, beliefs, attitudes, and perceptions. The following ideas may be explored:

1. People seem to attach different degrees of importance and significance to events and eras, related to whether they experienced those times directly or think of them as part of history.

2. One's current personal values, beliefs, attitudes, and perceptions result in part from the dominant social and economic conditions existing during the formative years in one's development.

3. Identical events have different meanings and different impact for different people.

4. Events, past and present, such as the Great Depression, World War II, President Kennedy's assassination, introduction of the birth-control pill, Woodstock, the war in Vietnam, the Watergate scandal, and so on, play a part in shaping the views and morals of all persons in a given era.

(Fifteen minutes.)

II. Each participant receives a copy of the Lifeline Work Sheet and a pencil. The facilitator gives instructions for completing the work sheet:

1. In the first column marked "Seven-Year Period," participants enter the year of their birth and the year in which they were age seven (e.g., 1942-1949). Below that, they enter the year that they reached the age of eight and the year that they reached the age of fourteen (e.g., 1950-1956). They continue to fill in the dates for each seven-year period of their lives. (Fifteen minutes.)

2. In the "Social Environment" column, participants enter events that were significant *for them* during the designated years. Participants may wish to include items such as political events, wars, technological advances, popular music, movies, books, sports events, and so on.

3. In the "Personal Life" column, participants list important events in their own lives or in the lives of persons close to them during the designated years. Examples include births, deaths, marriages, divorces, college, job changes, crises, travel, relationships, accomplishments, and the like.

III. The facilitator forms the participants into groups of four to six members each to share the information on their Lifeline Work Sheets. (The exchanges are most productive when each group includes persons of varied ages.) The participants are instructed to share information about:

1. Similarities and differences in their experiences and their significance.

2. Ways in which public events were experienced. An example might be the impact of the Watergate scandal on the members' faith in the political system.

3. How differences in backgrounds are seen as contributing to differences in values, perceptions, etc.

(Twenty minutes.)

IV. The facilitator then leads a discussion of the activity with the total group. The facilitator elicits a sampling of the variety of experiences present in the group, e.g., public events that have special meaning for group members, differences in experiences among participants in various age groups, and learnings about the ways in which differences in experiences contribute to conflicts and misunderstandings based on differing values, beliefs, perceptions, and attitudes. (Twenty minutes.)

V. The facilitator summarizes points made during the discussion and helps the participants to formulate generalizations about the impact of social issues on the formation of personal attitudes. (Ten minutes.)

VI. The participants are instructed to record their thoughts and the implications of their learnings to back-home situations. (Ten minutes.)

Variations

I. The entire group can brainstorm events to be listed in the "Social Environment" column.

II. Small groups can be formed according to a criterion such as sex, race, organizational role, or other salient aspect. The facilitator can decide in advance which criterion to use, or the total group can decide on a meaningful way to divide itself.

III. The total group can construct the lifeline of a "typical" group member, either before or after discussing individual lifelines.

IV. Particular members of the group—such as the oldest and the youngest—can share their responses in a group-on-group arrangement.

V. Participants can include on their work sheets the names of role models or "heroes" who were important to them at various ages.

Similar Structured Experiences: *Vol. I:* Structured Experience **20**; '73 *Annual:* **94**; '79 *Annual:* **233**.
Lecturette Source: '72 *Annual:* "Assumptions About the Nature of Man."

Notes on the Use of "Lifeline":

Submitted by Spencer H. Wyant.

LIFELINE WORK SHEET

Age	Seven-Year Period	Social Environment	Personal Life
Birth to 7			
8 to 14			
15 to 21			
22 to 28			
29 to 35			
36 to 42			
43 to 49			
50 to 56			
57 to 63			
64 to 70			

299. GROUP IDENTITY: A DEVELOPMENTAL PLANNING SESSION

Goals

I. To provide the members of an intact group with a model for understanding the factors that influence its development.

II. To enable the members of an intact group to identify its current stage of growth.

III. To promote group cohesiveness by exploring the needs and interests of its members.

Group Size

Any number of groups of five to eight members each.

Time Required

Approximately two hours.

Materials

I. A copy of the Group Identity Phases of Group Growth Sheet for each participant.

II. A copy of the Group Identity Work Sheet for each participant.

III. A pencil for each participant.

IV. A sheet of newsprint and a felt-tipped marker for each group.

V. Masking tape for each group.

Physical Setting

A room large enough to accommodate all members of an intact group, seated in a circle on the floor or around a circular table.

Process

I. The facilitator gives each participant a copy of the Group Identity Phases of Group Growth Sheet and presents a lecturette on the model. (Ten minutes.)

II. The facilitator discusses the goals of the activity and outlines its steps. (Five minutes.)

III. The facilitator distributes the Group Identity Work Sheets and pencils, divides the participants into groups of five to eight members each, and directs the members to fill in their work sheets. (Five to ten minutes.)

IV. Subgroup members share and clarify their written responses. (Fifteen to twenty minutes.)

V. Newsprint, felt-tipped markers, and masking tape are distributed, and groups are directed to develop group identity posters. These are to be descriptive statements that reflect predominant individual and group needs as well as the purpose (task) of the group. (Thirty minutes.)

VI. Subgroup posters are shared with all participants. (Five minutes.)

VII. The facilitator instructs the subgroup members to reflect on the posters they have created and the model of group development presented earlier and to determine which phase of development the group is in at this point. (Ten minutes.)

VIII. Groups are directed to discuss strategies for achieving Phase IV of group growth (a balance between individual, group, and task needs). (Fifteen to twenty minutes.)

IX. The total group is reconvened, and one reporter from each group discusses the group's developmental phase and its strategies for achieving group growth. (Ten to twenty minutes.)

X. The facilitator elicits comments about the experience and briefly summarizes the learnings, emphasizing general themes and applications of the concepts presented.

Variations

I. A recorder can be designated to post key words and ideas during step IV. This list can then serve as a guideline for developing the statement of group identity in step V.

II. The activity can be used with groups that are not intact or ongoing by using the subgroupings and presenting the task as an exploration of how the concepts apply to nonwork groups or in starting up a new work team. Instructions in step VIII are then related to planning for the group's needs if it were to continue to meet or if members were to work together on a project.

III. The activity can be used as an intermittent processing activity to help ongoing work groups review their processes.

Similar Structured Experiences: *Vol. II:* Structured Experience 39; *Vol. III: 66*; *'74 Annual:* **126**; *Vol. VI:* **208.**

Suggested Instrument: '77 *Annual:* "TORI Group Self-Diagnosis Scale."

Lecturette Sources: '73 *Annual:* "A Model of Group Development"; '74 *Annual:* "Cog's Ladder: A Model of Group Development"; '77 *Annual:* "D-I-D: A Three-Dimensional Model for Understanding Group Communication."

Notes on the Use of "Group Identity":

Submitted by Kenneth W. Howard.

GROUP IDENTITY PHASES OF GROUP GROWTH SHEET[1]

During every group interaction, three types of needs are present: individual needs, group needs, and task needs. The length of time spent on each type of need depends on many variables, a major one being the phase of group development.

I (Personal Needs): Becoming oriented to the group, finding out whether one's personal needs will be met

WE (Group Needs): Developing useful membership roles, ground rules, procedures, and group structures as needs emerge

IT (Group Task): Focusing on the agreed-on objective(s)

The following diagram depicts different stages in the evolution of a group:

Relative length of time spent on each type of need (by phase):

Phase I: Orientation, Testing, and Dependency

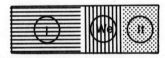

Phase II: Organizing to Get Work Done, Intragroup Conflict

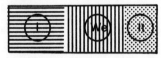

Phase III: Information Flow, Group Cohesion

Phase IV: Problem Solving, Interdependence

[1]Reprinted from Ann R. Bauman, *Training of Trainers: Resource Manual,* National Drug Abuse Center, Washington, D C , 1977. Used with permission.

GROUP IDENTITY WORK SHEET

Instructions: Complete the following statements individually.

1. The personal needs that I have as they relate to being a member of this group are:

2. My perceptions of the needs that we share as members of this group are:

3. The primary purpose for this group's existence is:

4. Our task as a group is to:

300. PROJECTIONS: INTERPERSONAL AWARENESS EXPANSION

Goals

  I. To help participants to explore the process of projection.

 II. To provide an opportunity for participants to recognize how and what they project about others.

III. To enable participants to become more aware of the part they play in the outcome of unpleasant situations.

Group Size

Any number of groups of four to six members each.

Time Required

One and one-half hours.

Materials

  I. A copy of the Projections Feelings Identification Sheet for each participant.

 II. One or more copies of the Projections Situation Analysis Sheet for each participant.

III. A copy of the Projections Processing Sheet for each participant.

IV. A pencil for each participant.

Physical Setting

A room that is large enough for individual writing and small-group discussions.

Process

  I. The facilitator explains the goals of the activity and gives a brief lecturette on the process of projection. He may define projection and related terms; e.g., *projection* is the assumption that what is true for oneself is also true for others: "You must be sad (angry, frustrated) about that," "He looks bored." The facilitator stresses that the focus of the experience is on identifying ways that participants *project* feelings, ideas, or values onto others and on how this process affects interactions. (Twenty minutes.)

II. Each participant receives a copy of the Projections Feelings Identification Sheet, a copy of the Projections Situation Analysis Sheet, and a pencil.

III. Each participant is directed to work independently on the Projections Feelings Identification Sheet and to identify a person in his or her life (including anyone in the group) whom the participant feels rejected by, disliked by, or criticized by, or who makes the participant feel uneasy or uncomfortable. (Ten minutes.)

IV. The participants are instructed to select one (or more) situation(s) to analyze. A separate Projections Situation Analysis Sheet is used for each situation. (Ten minutes.)

V. The facilitator calls time and distributes a copy of the Projections Processing Sheet to each participant. Members take ten minutes to fill these out.

VI. The participants are divided into groups of four to six members each and are directed to share their responses to the processing questions within their small groups. Subgroup members help to clarify each other's learnings. (Twenty minutes.)

VII. The entire group is assembled, and a reporter from each small group summarizes the learnings that were described during the processing discussion. The facilitator helps to clarify key learnings related to the goals of the experience. (Ten minutes.)

VIII. The facilitator leads a discussion of ways in which an increased awareness of projections can be used constructively in the future. (Ten minutes.)

Variations

I. If the participants are members of intact groups, the activity can focus exclusively on other group members, and a follow-up activity can be conducted to help the two partners discuss the issues involved.

II. Helping partners, or persons with whom participants feel comfortable, can be used instead of small groups during step VI.

III. Participants can reconvene within their small groups to generate strategies for applying their learnings during step VIII.

Similar Structured Experiences: *Vol. IV:* Structured Experience **106**; *Vol. V:* **131**; '76 *Annual:* **180**; *Vol. VI:* **214**.

Suggested Instruments: '72 *Annual:* "Interpersonal Relationship Rating Scale"; '74 *Annual:* "Self-Disclosure Questionnaire"; '77 *Annual:* "Interpersonal Check List (ICL)"; '80 *Annual:* "Personal Style Inventory."

Lecturette Source: '76 *Annual:* "The Awareness Wheel."

Notes on the Use of "Projections":

Submitted by Bernard Nisenholz.

PROJECTIONS FEELINGS IDENTIFICATION SHEET

Using the following items as a guide, identify one or more persons who fit at least one of the categories. Fill in as many names and/or categories as you feel represent an authentic response for you.

1. I feel rejected by (answer may be specific or general, e.g., Sam, authority figures, my mother)

2. I feel uneasy with

3. I feel disliked by

4. I feel criticized by

5. I feel frustrated by

PROJECTIONS SITUATION ANALYSIS SHEET

Instructions: Review your responses on the Projections Feelings Identification Sheet. Select one situation to analyze. (If time permits, you may be asked to analyze one or more of the other situations.)

Your feeling ⎯⎯⎯⎯⎯⎯⎯⎯⎯⎯⎯⎯⎯⎯⎯⎯⎯⎯⎯⎯⎯⎯⎯⎯

Name of the person involved in the situation with you ⎯⎯⎯⎯⎯⎯⎯⎯⎯⎯

Consider the following aspects of a typical interaction with this person:

The person's actual behavior

. . . tone of voice

. . . choice of words

. . . use of gestures

. . . relevant nonverbal cues

Setting: When does this usually occur?

Where?

Who is typically present?

Issue: What appears to be at stake?

What does either of you stand to win or lose?

What do you assume to be the other person's motive?

Other important aspects:

PROJECTIONS PROCESSING SHEET

1. Review the notes you made on the Projections Situation Analysis Sheet. Identify your typical behavior in this situation in terms of each of the aspects considered. Try to identify the part you are responsible for, e.g., "He rejects me by telling me only negative things, and I believe them."

2. How do you feel during this interaction? How does that contribute to the negative outcome?

3. How many of these identified behaviors that others do to you, do you also do to yourself (e.g., if you feel rejected by someone else for being assertive, do you reject yourself for that also)?

4. Are you doing to this person (people) the thing that you accuse this person (people) of doing to you?

5. *Complete the following notes to yourself:* One of the learnings that I am gaining about the ways in which my feelings and behavior contribute to unpleasant situations with others is . . .

301. RESISTANCE TO LEARNING: DEVELOPING NEW SKILLS

Goals

I. To provide a model for understanding the phenomenon of behavioral resistance in learning situations.

II. To demonstrate various behavioral manifestations of resistance.

III. To increase awareness of techniques that can be used to overcome resistance in learning situations.

Group Size

Any number of groups of five to seven members each.

Time Required

Two hours.

Materials

I. A copy of the Resistance to Learning Work Sheet for each participant.

II. Blank paper and a pencil for each participant.

III. Newsprint and a felt-tipped marker for each group.

IV. Masking tape for each group.

Physical Setting

A room large enough to accommodate the groups comfortably, and tables with chairs, or circles of chairs, for each group.

Process

I. The facilitator introduces the activity and explains the goals. (Five minutes.)

II. The facilitator introduces the concept of a passive-to-active continuum of resistance to new learnings and unfamiliar situations and discusses the benefits of learning to identify and cope with one's own personal style of resistance. The Resistance to Learning Work Sheets and pencils are distributed to the participants. (Ten minutes.)

III. The participants are directed to complete the "personal resistance behaviors" portion of the work sheet, identifying passive and active manifestations of their own resistances. (Ten minutes.)

IV. Groups of five to seven members each are formed and assigned the task of developing summaries of the group members' identifications of resistant behaviors. Newsprint, felt-tipped markers, and masking tape are distributed to the groups so the summaries can be listed and posted. (Ten minutes.)

V. One member from each work group displays the group's poster for all participants to see. (Five minutes.)

VI. The facilitator creates a new, summary poster that eliminates duplication from the group lists and represents the major or typical resistance behaviors identified by the participants. (Ten minutes.)

VII. The facilitator gives a brief lecturette on typical behaviors that exemplify attempts to manage personal and interpersonal resistance and gives examples of both covert and overt behaviors. (Five minutes.)

VIII. The participants are directed to work individually to complete the "resistance-management behaviors" section of their Resistance to Learning Work Sheets. (Five minutes.)

IX. The small groups are reassembled, and the members are instructed to share their responses as before and develop a group summary of typical behaviors used to manage resistance. Clean newsprint is provided. (Ten minutes.)

X. Group posters are presented, as before. (Five minutes.)

XI. The facilitator prepares a new summary report, eliminating duplicates from the group lists. The facilitator then leads a discussion of members' responses to the resistance-management behaviors that have been identified. Additional strategies for managing resistance are elicited, and the facilitator adds strategies to the list as appropriate. (Fifteen minutes.)

XII. Each participant is given blank paper and is directed to identify a particular resistance behavior that has created problems in new learning situations in the past and to state an action that the participant can take to manage the resistance more effectively in the future. (Ten minutes.)

XIII. The subgroups are reassembled and further divided into dyads or triads. The members' action plans are then shared, with the partners serving as resources in clarifying the action plans discussed. (Ten to fifteen minutes.)

XIV. The facilitator reconvenes the total group to provide an opportunity for members to give comments and reactions to the activity and also to reiterate effective techniques for managing resistance to learning. (Ten minutes.)

Variations

I. Each group can conduct a skit depicting resistance. The other groups then develop a response to the resistance.

II. The participants can be instructed to identify resistance to new learning in specific situations such as skills acquisition, new social groupings, new cultural settings, etc.

III. Further analysis of personal resistance can be effected by identifying factors that influence movement along the continuum from active to passive resistance and from covert to overt management of resistance.

IV. More detailed action plans for effective management of personal resistance can be developed, with evaluation of efforts and follow-through procedures specified.

V. With intact groups, a feedback element can be added as an aspect of the small-group sharing. Group members can comment on the effects of their resistance behaviors and serve as resources to each other in helping to identify additional resistance behaviors.

Lecturette Sources: *'79 Annual:* "The Emotional Cycle of Change," "Transactions in the Change Process."

Notes on the Use of "Resistance to Learning":

Submitted by Hyler Bracey and Roy Trueblood.

RESISTANCE TO LEARNING WORK SHEET

My Personal Resistance Behaviors

Passive   Active

My Resistance-Management Behaviors

Covert   Overt

302. CROSS-GROUP NEGOTIATION AND COOPERATION: STUDYING GROUP DYNAMICS

Goals

I. To provide an opportunity to experience the effects of cooperation in task-group functioning.

II. To explore the effects of conflicting objectives on the behavior of members of a task group.

III. To increase awareness of the positive effects of planning, negotiation, and sharing of resources among work-group members.

Group Size

Two to six groups of four members each.

Time Required

Approximately one and one-half hours.

Materials

I. A copy of the appropriate Cross-Group Negotiation and Cooperation Instruction Sheet for each group member.

II. A large box of Tinkertoys® (350 pieces) for each group.

III. Newsprint and a felt-tipped marker.

Physical Setting

A room large enough to allow the groups to work separately, preferably on the floor.

Process

I. The facilitator divides the participants into groups of four members each and instructs the groups to assign a number to each member by counting off.

II. The facilitator gives each group a set of Tinkertoys and gives each participant a copy of the appropriate Cross-Group Negotiation and Cooperation Instruction Sheet, i.e., member 1 in each group receives instruction sheet 1, etc.

III. The facilitator announces that the members have twenty-five minutes in which to complete all their tasks.

IV. The facilitator calls time and directs each group to display its constructions.

V. The entire group is reassembled, and the members share their reactions to the activity and then discuss their experiences by reviewing the following points:

1. Did each group complete all the tasks assigned?
2. How did each group decide the order for completing the tasks? Was a plan for accomplishing all the tasks discussed?
3. Which task was easiest for members to accomplish? Which was most difficult?
4. Which task gave the most satisfaction? Which task gave the least satisfaction?
5. How were information and resources shared within the groups?

(Twenty minutes.)

VI. The facilitator helps to summarize the main points from the general discussion and reconvenes the work groups to process the learnings. Group members are directed to discuss the experience by focusing on the following questions:

1. What did members learn from their group's functioning? What did participants learn about their own behavior as members of a group?
2. What would members do differently if they had to repeat the activity?

(Fifteen minutes.)

VII. The facilitator calls for a report of key learnings from each subgroup. (Ten minutes.)

VIII. Group members are instructed to develop applications of their learnings to their back-home situations. (Ten minutes.)

Variations

I. Participants can be informed that they are competing with other groups. The task processes can be timed or completed structures can be judged on aesthetics, stability, or creativity.

II. Larger subgroups can be formed with more than one member receiving the same set of instructions.

III. When working with intact work groups, an additional discussion question can be added during step VIII to help group members apply their learnings to improve their intragroup cooperation.

IV. Work-group composition can be based on specific criteria such as job description, sex, etc.

Similar Structured Experiences: '72 *Annual:* Structured Experience **78**; *Vol. V:* **150**; *Vol. VII:* **263**.
Lecturette Source: '73 *Annual:* "Win/Lose Situations."

Notes on the Use of "Cross-Group Negotiation and Cooperation":

Submitted by Barbara L. Fisher and Roberta G. Sachs.

CROSS-GROUP NEGOTIATION AND COOPERATION
INSTRUCTION SHEETS

For Group Member 1:

1. Complete a Tinkertoy structure with someone outside your group.
2. Complete a Tinkertoy structure with one other person in your group.
3. Complete a Tinkertoy structure by yourself.
4. Complete a Tinkertoy structure with your entire group.

For Group Member 2:

1. Complete a Tinkertoy structure by yourself.
2. Complete a Tinkertoy structure with your entire group.
3. Complete a Tinkertoy structure with someone outside your group.
4. Complete a Tinkertoy structure with one other person in your group.

For Group Member 3:

1. Complete a Tinkertoy structure with one other person in your group.
2. Complete a Tinkertoy structure by yourself.
3. Complete a Tinkertoy structure with your entire group.
4. Complete a Tinkertoy structure with someone outside your group.

For Group Member 4:

1. Complete a Tinkertoy structure with your entire group.
2. Complete a Tinkertoy structure with someone outside your group.
3. Complete a Tinkertoy structure with one other person in your group.
4. Complete a Tinkertoy structure by yourself.

---

303. DEVELOPING TRUST: A LEADERSHIP SKILL

Goals

I. To examine some of the behaviors and personal qualities that affect the process of establishing trust in relationships.

II. To analyze current behaviors and attitudes related to establishing trust in relationships.

III. To increase awareness of how one is perceived by others in regard to behaviors that enhance the building of trust.

Group Size

Approximately six to twenty-four participants.

Time Required

Approximately two hours.

Materials

I. A copy of the Developing Trust Analysis Sheet for each participant.

II. A copy of the Developing Trust Inventory Sheet (Self) for each participant.

III. One or more copies of the Developing Trust Inventory Sheet (Other) for each participant.

IV. A pencil for each participant.

Physical Setting

A room large enough for participants to move about freely and conduct semiprivate discussions.

Process

I. The facilitator briefly discusses the goals of the activity and the general importance of trust in effective interpersonal relationships. (Five minutes.)

II. The facilitator distributes one copy of the Developing Trust Analysis Sheet and a pencil to each participant and instructs the group members to follow the instructions provided. (Ten minutes.)

III. The facilitator divides the participants into small groups of three or four members each and instructs them to discuss their rankings of the items on the Developing Trust Analysis Sheet. (Ten minutes.)

IV. The subgroups are disbanded, and the facilitator distributes a copy of the Developing Trust Inventory Sheet (Self) to each participant. Each participant is instructed to complete the form and put it aside for later use. (Five minutes.)

V. The facilitator distributes a copy of the Developing Trust Inventory Sheet (Other) to each participant and instructs each member to find a partner.

VI. The members of the dyads work independently to complete the Developing Trust Inventory Sheet (Other) with regard to their partners. (Five minutes.)

VII. Inventories are exchanged between partners and the ratings are discussed. As time permits, this process can be repeated one or more times. A new Developing Trust Inventory Sheet (Other) is used for each new pairing. (Five minutes.)

VIII. After all data from the partners have been collected and shared, the participants are instructed to work independently to compare their self-appraisal data with the scores they received from others. (Five minutes.)

IX. The participants are directed to return to their original discussion groups to debrief the activity. (Fifteen minutes.)

X. After each subgroup member has had an opportunity to discuss some of the significant aspects of the activity, the facilitator instructs the participants to focus on key learnings they have had regarding their current functioning in establishing trust in relationships. Subgroup members can take turns completing the sentence "Something I learned/relearned/am in the process of learning about trust is . . . ." (Fifteen minutes.)

XI. Subgroup members then are directed to work independently to develop behavioral goals to increase their effectiveness in establishing trust in relationships. (Ten minutes.)

XII. The subgroups are reconvened and the members are directed to read their goals and to help each other clarify and refine them if necessary. (Fifteen minutes.)

Variations

I. The feedback step can be eliminated. Participants then use self-appraisal data as the source from which developmental goals are generated.

II. Participants can generate all or some of the components and follow the scaling and group procedures as outlined.

III. Group or subgroup comparisons profiling the rankings can be generated by the facilitator during step III.

IV. When working with intact work groups, the data shared during step III can be discussed in terms of their implications for group functioning.

V. Participants can average all the scores they received from others in order to determine a "Trust Inventory Index." This index can be compared with subsequent scores obtained at a later date to help evaluate progress in trust relations.

Similar Structured Experiences: *Vol. IV:* Structured Experience **120**; *Vol. VI:* **216**.

Suggested Instruments: *Vol. I:* "T-P Leadership Questionnaire"; '72 *Annual:* "Supervisory Attitudes: The X-Y Scale"; '73 *Annual:* "LEAD (Leadership: Employee-Orientation and Differentiation) Questionnaire"; '76 *Annual:* "Leader Effectiveness and Adaptability Description (LEAD)."

Lecturette Sources: '77 *Annual:* "A Practical Leadership Paradigm"; '79 *Annual:* "The Centered Boss."

Notes on the Use of "Developing Trust":

Submitted by William J. Bailey.

DEVELOPING TRUST ANALYSIS SHEET

Name

Current theories and research concerning leadership stress the situational aspects of leadership effectiveness. In other words, a leader must take into account the particular dynamics of the organization, the existing social conditions, the characteristics of the followers, and his or her own leadership style. This means that effective leadership cannot be viewed as an isolated component. Leadership is relative, subjective, and interactive.

One component of leadership that appears to be germane to all leadership roles is "relating." Relating, as a leadership skill, involves a variety of behaviors, including a particularly important one: establishing trust relationships.

Some of the behaviors and qualities involved in establishing a climate of trust are:

- Sharing (the sharing of personal events, e.g., family matters, feelings)
- Vulnerability (the extent to which the leader is perceived as having the capacity to be vulnerable, i.e., to err is human)
- Loyalty (commitment to consistent goals of the organization and its leaders)
- Accepting others (accepting the unique behavior of others)
- Involving others (using others for input or decision making)
- Valuing (willingness to exchange ideas and ideals with others)
- Awareness (sensitivity to the needs of others)
- Communicating (giving clear communications, both oral and written)
- Openness (willingness to explore new experiences)
- Honesty (avoidance of deceit)

Take a few minutes right now to think about these items. You will probably become aware that some of the items on the list mean more to you than others. You may want to add to the list.

In order to become aware of the relative importance of these items to you, rank them from one to ten (one representing the most important item). If you add items to the list, you may include them in your ranking.

	Behavior or Quality	Why You Ranked It this Way
1.	_____	
2.	_____	
3.	_____	
4.	_____	
5.	_____	
6.	_____	
7.	_____	
8.	_____	
9.	_____	
10.	_____	
Other	_____	

Be prepared to discuss your reactions to the items and your rationale for the rankings you have given the items.

DEVELOPING TRUST INVENTORY SHEET (SELF)

Consider each of the components of establishing trust in relationships in turn. Give yourself a score, based on the following rating scale, that best describes *your* behavior to most people, most of the time, at this time in your life.

Points	Meaning
1	The behavior is exhibited consistently (most of the time)
2	The behavior is exhibited frequently (much of the time)
3	The behavior is inconsistent (sometimes yes, sometimes no)
4	The behavior is exhibited infrequently (sometimes)
5	The behavior is seldom exhibited (very little)

Component	Your Rating
Sharing	
Vulnerability	
Loyalty	
Accepting Others	
Involving Others	
Valuing	
Awareness	
Communicating	
Openness	
Honesty	
Other	

DEVELOPING TRUST INVENTORY SHEET (OTHER)

Points	*Meaning*
1	The behavior is exhibited consistently (most of the time)
2	The behavior is exhibited frequently (much of the time)
3	The behavior is inconsistent (sometimes yes, sometimes no)
4	The behavior is exhibited infrequently (sometimes)
5	The behavior is seldom exhibited (very little)

Component	Perceptions from Other
Sharing	
Vulnerability	
Loyalty	
Accepting Others	
Involving Others	
Valuing	
Awareness	
Communicating	
Openness	
Honesty	
Other	

304. WHEN TO DELEGATE: A MANAGER'S DILEMMA

Goals

    I. To provide an opportunity to exchange views on the topic of delegation.

    II. To increase awareness of attitudes about task delegation.

Group Size

    Two or more groups of five to seven members each.

Time Required

    Two and one-half to three hours.

Materials

    I. A copy of the When to Delegate Inventory Sheet for each participant.

    II. A pencil for each participant.

    III. Newsprint and a felt-tipped marker for each group.

    IV. Masking tape.

Physical Setting

    A room large enough for each group to work without interfering with the other groups, or several small rooms adjacent to each other. A table and chairs for each group.

Process

    I. The facilitator introduces the activity as one that will enable the participants to do some critical analytical thinking and then to pool and integrate group ideas and experience on the subject of delegation. The facilitator gives each participant a copy of the When to Delegate Inventory Sheet and a pencil. (Five minutes.)

    II. The participants are directed to read the inventory sheet and to determine, for each of the items on the sheet, those situations in which delegation is advisable, those in which it is not, and those situations in which delegation is not relevant. Members are counseled that they should consider the organization's needs and policies, as well as the individual's own career interests, in making these selections. (Fifteen minutes.)

III. The facilitator forms subgroups of five to seven members each. Each group is given newsprint and a felt-tipped marker and is told that it has forty minutes to develop two lists: one for situations in which delegation is advisable, and one for situations in which it is not. The facilitator stresses the importance of using a procedure for reaching consensus on items for the list without "averaging" or "majority-rule" voting, i.e., the group's list should include only those items on which there is substantial agreement. The groups are directed to write their lists on the newsprint sheets and to post them.

IV. After forty minutes, all participants are encouraged to stroll around and look at the other groups' lists. (Ten minutes.)

V. The facilitator assembles all participants and leads a discussion of the pros and cons of delegation as a managerial style. The "answers" can be posted on newsprint. (Fifteen minutes.)

VI. Subgroups are re-formed and instructed to examine their lists to identify the themes and biases underlying the placement of various items, including any new thoughts there may be on individual items or the lists in general. (Ten to fifteen minutes.)

VII. Subgroups are instructed to process the experience in the following manner:
   1. Going around the group, members briefly discuss experiences related to the issue of delegation as a managerial tool.
   2. Each group member, in turn, briefly states what he has learned, relearned, or is becoming more aware of as a result of the activity.

   (Twenty-five minutes.)

VIII. Participants are encouraged to devise ways of using their new insights in their back-home work situations. The subgroup members act as helpers to develop practical applications (e.g., role playing can be used to help a member who feels trapped in a situation, brainstorming can be used to provide fresh ideas to help another member out of a dilemma, and so on). (Twenty minutes.)

IX. A reporter from each subgroup shares with the large group the best ideas or insights developed by the subgroups. (Fifteen minutes.)

Variations

I. A lecturette on delegation can be given prior to the experiential learning activity.

II. Readings can be assigned to group members prior to the structured experience to expose participants to various theories and/or viewpoints that will be explored in the discussions.

Structured Experience   304

III. After completing the inventory sheet, participants can be instructed to review their responses to the twenty items in terms of the type of managerial attitudes they expect of their subordinates. This content can then be discussed during step VIII.

IV. Subgroup members can develop lists of pros and cons to be shared with the large group during step VII. The facilitator then focuses on themes that have emerged across subgroup lists and adds input based on managerial theory, if appropriate.

Similar Structured Experience: *Vol. I:* Structured Experience **3.**

Suggested Instruments: '72 *Annual:* "Supervisory Attitudes: The X-Y Scale"; '73 *Annual:* "LEAD (Leadership: Employee Orientation and Differentiation) Questionnaire"; '80 *Annual:* "Increasing Employee Self-Control (IESC)."

Lecturette Sources: '72 *Annual:* "McGregor's Theory X-Theory Y Model"; '75 *Annual:* "Participatory Management: A New Morality"; '77 *Annual:* "A Practical Leadership Paradigm."

Notes on the Use of "When to Delegate":

Submitted by T. F. Carney.

WHEN TO DELEGATE INVENTORY SHEET

Instructions: Below are listed a variety of features of a job situation. Some features suggest that delegation is clearly advisable ("yes"). Some features suggest that it would not be advisable to delegate ("no"). Yet other features are not directly related to the issue of delegation ("does not apply").

Individually, read over the items that follow and:

1. Identify situations in which the manager would be best advised to delegate tasks (including providing for the training of subordinates).
2. Identify situations in which it would *not* be in the manager's best interests to delegate or to train someone to take over a task.
3. Identify situations that you think are not related to the issue of delegation or are misleading—based on erroneous judgments about delegating (for example, a false assumption that a certain procedure should *necessarily* precede, go with, or follow delegation).

Be as clear as possible in your own mind about why you have included an item in any category. Try to apply management theory in placing the items in the different categories.

Features of your job situation:

1. The firm does not have a human resource development policy and goes in for firefighting.

    ☐ yes   ☐ no   ☐ does not apply

2. Your top subordinate wants your job and is keen to push you out of it.

    ☐ yes   ☐ no   ☐ does not apply

3. You have good skills in coordinating all aspects of your job.

    ☐ yes   ☐ no   ☐ does not apply

4. You do not want to become unpopular with your subordinates by giving out tough assignments, since you will have to demote them if they do not perform well. If you delegate tasks, it will serve as a test of your subordinates' abilities.

    ☐ yes   ☐ no   ☐ does not apply

5. In your firm, mistakes are held against you—and you are supposed to know the details of what is going on in your section.

    ☐ yes   ☐ no   ☐ does not apply

6. Some job openings are scheduled to come up next year, at the next level up from where you are now.

    ☐ yes   ☐ no   ☐ does not apply

7. The company is in a steady-state/zero-personnel-growth situation.

☐ yes   ☐ no   ☐ does not apply

8. The company is in a fast-growth business situation.

☐ yes   ☐ no   ☐ does not apply

9. There are wide disparities in the abilities of your subordinates, and delegation will widen gaps still further because your top performers will get experience in key tasks.

☐ yes   ☐ no   ☐ does not apply

10. This phase of your company's product growth requires risk taking and innovation, but the competition is also moving fast, so time will be a key factor in your attempts at product development.

☐ yes   ☐ no   ☐ does not apply

11. Traditionally in your firm, subordinates take difficult tasks to the manager; it is the manager's job to come up with solutions.

☐ yes   ☐ no   ☐ does not apply

12. You need more time to concentrate on the key aspects of your job and to make better connections at your level in management. You could use more new ideas from inside your department.

☐ yes   ☐ no   ☐ does not apply

13. You are a perfectionist about your work. If you delegate, you know that you will have to assume responsibility for any errors made.

☐ yes   ☐ no   ☐ does not apply

14. You are a management-by-objectives and critical-path whiz, you read about time management just out of interest, and you have identified the 20 percent of your job that is going to give you the maximum payoff and visibility.

☐ yes   ☐ no   ☐ does not apply

15. There is *one* outstanding person among your subordinates who could develop rapidly to a stage where he could do your job at least as well as you can.

☐ yes   ☐ no   ☐ does not apply

16. You have no experience in delegating or follow-up checking procedures.

☐ yes   ☐ no   ☐ does not apply

17. The firm operates with replacement charts and requires managers to train their successors and "bring new staff along." In particular, higher management does not want to be dependent on any *one* person.

☐ yes   ☐ no   ☐ does not apply

18. You are afraid that someone will overshadow you in doing your job and that you will not be perceived as essential to the operation of your unit.

    □ yes   □ no   □ does not apply

19. You are facing a task in which, if you make the wrong decision, there will be *very* serious consequences for your entire operation.

    □ yes   □ no   □ does not apply

20. There are a lot of really bright young people in your department. If you delegate heavily to them, they might gain enough experience to leave you for promotion opportunities elsewhere in the organization.

    □ yes   □ no   □ does not apply

305. SEXISM IN ADVERTISEMENTS: EXPLORING STEREOTYPES

Goals

   I. To become more aware of sex-role stereotyping in advertisements.

  II. To identify elements of advertisements that do or do not reflect sex-role stereotyping.

 III. To increase awareness of the effects of social conditioning.

Group Size

Three or more groups of four to six members each.

Time Required

Approximately one and one-half hours.

Materials

Newsprint and a felt-tipped marker for each participant.

Physical Setting

A room large enough for each group to meet without disturbing the other groups, and a writing surface for each participant.

Process

   I. The facilitator introduces the activity but does not state the goals. The facilitator distributes newsprint and a felt-tipped marker to each participant and instructs each member to design a one-page advertisement to be used in a popular magazine. Specifications for the ad are:
   1. To promote the ease of using a coffee maker
   2. Showing one, three, or five people
   3. In an office setting.
   (Ten minutes.)

  II. The facilitator calls time and divides the participants into groups of four to six members each.

III. The facilitator directs the members to share their ads and then to debrief the design task by discussing within their groups the thoughts, hesitations, and conflicts they may have experienced while designing the advertisements. (Fifteen minutes.)

IV. The facilitator directs each group to design a new advertisement that will be presented to the large group. The new ad is to reflect group members' views on the most effective approach to use in selling the product. (Ten minutes.)

V. Each group presents its ad to the total membership. Rationales for the new ads are shared at this time. (Fifteen minutes.)

VI. The facilitator leads a discussion of the members' reactions to the ads presented. Participants are instructed to consider the ads with respect to sex-role stereotyping. (Ten minutes.)

VII. The facilitator helps group members develop a list of characteristics of ads that reinforce existing sex-role stereotypes. (Ten minutes.)

VIII. The facilitator makes a brief statement about the role of social conditioning in the perpetuation of sex-role stereotyping. (Five minutes.)

IX. The participants are instructed to work independently to complete the following sentences:

1. I am programmed to see men/women as . . .
2. I am conditioned to see myself as . . .

(Five minutes.)

X. The design groups are reconvened and are directed to discuss their responses to the sentences and to clarify action steps they can take to overcome their perceptual biases and to combat sex-role stereotyping. (Fifteen minutes.)

Variations

I. Groups of participants can be directed to produce one-minute television advertisements (skits) instead of magazine advertisements.

II. The facilitator can focus attention on stereotyping processes in general rather than on sex-role stereotyping in particular.

III. All-male, all-female, and mixed-sex subgroups can be established for step II. The similarities and differences in the groups' ads can then be considered during step VI.

Similar Structured Experiences: '76 *Annual:* Structured Experience **184**; *Vol. VII:* **258**.

Suggested Instruments: '73 *Annual:* "Sex-Role Stereotyping Rating Scale"; '77 *Annual:* "Bem Sex-Role Inventory (BSRI)"; '79 *Annual:* "Women as Managers Scale (WAMS)."
Lecturette Source: '77 *Annual:* "Androgyny."

Notes on the Use of "Sexism in Advertisements":

Submitted by Anne J. Burr, Deborah C. L. Griffith, David B. Lyon, Gertrude E. Philpot, Gary N. Powell, and Dorianne L. Sehring.

306. PRAISE: GIVING AND RECEIVING POSITIVE FEEDBACK

Goals

   I. To develop an awareness of one's own accomplishments.

   II. To practice giving public recognition to others.

   III. To become aware of one's responses to recognition from others.

Group Size

   Any number of dyads.

Time Required

   One and one-half to two hours.

Materials

   I. Blank paper and a pencil for each participant.

   II. Newsprint and a felt-tipped marker.

Physical Setting

   A room in which all dyads can converse without disrupting each other.

Process

   I. The facilitator explains the goals of the activity. He discusses the importance of reward and recognition from others and the effect of these factors on self-concept, motivation, and behavior. (Five minutes.)

   II. Each participant is given blank paper and a pencil and is instructed to compose a list of:
      1. Two things I do well
      2. A recent major success or accomplishment
      3. A brief statement that I would like to have said about me.
      (Five to ten minutes.)

   III. The participants are directed to pair off and, in turn, exchange the information on their lists, clarifying and broadening whenever possible. (Ten minutes.)

IV. Each member is then instructed to compose a letter of recognition to his partner, based on the information received during step III. The letter is to be written directly to the partner, not to a third party. (Five minutes.)

V. The partners are directed to exchange letters, to read their letters, and to reflect on the contents without talking. (Five minutes.)

VI. The entire group is reassembled, and the members are told that they will have the opportunity to introduce and recommend their partners to the group. Each member, in turn, stands behind his partner, with his hands on the other's shoulders, and praises the partner to the other group members. The person being introduced does not comment at this time. (Two minutes each.)

VII. After all members have been introduced, individuals are given the opportunity to clarify any information given about themselves. (Two minutes each.)

VIII. The facilitator briefly states the idea that what one person says about another tells as much about the speaker. He suggests that the participants reflect on how their own values were evidenced by their presentations of their partners.

IX. The facilitator reconvenes the dyads and instructs them to debrief the activity by discussing their physical responses and behaviors as well as their feelings about the written and oral portions of the activity. (Ten minutes.)

X. The facilitator then instructs the partners to discuss what they learned about themselves during the activity. (Ten minutes.)

XI. The large group is reconvened. The facilitator calls for generalized statements about factors that influenced giving and receiving praise. (Ten minutes.)

XII. The group members are encouraged to relate this experience to their relationships with others and to suggest practical applications of their learnings to various back-home situations. (Five minutes.)

Variations

I. After being introduced verbally, members can read the lists they gave to their partners at the start of the activity to the entire group.

II. Members can read the letters written to them by their partners instead of being verbally introduced by them to the group.

III. Members can add additional information about themselves during step VII.

IV. During step V, oral praise can be exchanged to complement the letters.

Similar Structured Experiences: *Vol. I:* Structured Experience **20**; *'73 Annual:* **87**; *Vol. IV:* **104**; *'76 Annual:* **181**; *Vol. VI:* **197**.

Suggested Instruments: '74 *Annual:* "Self-Disclosure Questionnaire," "Interpersonal Communication Inventory"; '76 *Annual:* "Inventory of Self-Actualizing Characteristics (ISAC)."

Lecturette Sources: '74 *Annual:* "Five Components Contributing to Effective Interpersonal Communication"; '76 *Annual:* "Interpersonal Feedback as Consensual Validation of Constructs."

Notes on the Use of "Praise":

Submitted by Thomas J. Mason.

307. MAZE: ONE-WAY AND TWO-WAY COMMUNICATION

Goals

   I. To experience the effects of free versus restricted communication in accomplishing a task.

   II. To explore the impact of communication processes on the development of trust between a leader and a follower.

Group Size

Three to ten dyads and one additional person to serve as scorekeeper.

Time Required

Approximately one and one-half to two hours.

Materials

   I. A copy of the Maze Rules Sheet for the scorekeeper and for each leader.

   II. A copy of the Maze Score Sheet for the scorekeeper.

   III. A blindfold (a large, dark handkerchief or scarf can be used) for each leader.

   IV. A watch with a second hand or a stopwatch for the scorekeeper.

   V. A pencil for the scorekeeper.

Physical Setting

A room in which the activity can be introduced and processed and a large, adjacent room with twenty-eight movable chairs arranged to form a maze, as follows:

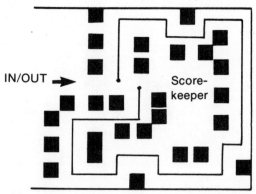

Process

I. The facilitator presents a lecturette on the importance of active involvement and communication in developing trust. (Five minutes.)

II. One member of the group is selected to serve as scorekeeper. The scorekeeper receives a copy of the Maze Rules Sheet, a copy of the Maze Score Sheet, a watch with which to time the activity, and a pencil.

III. The facilitator divides the remaining participants into dyads, preferably composed of members who are unfamiliar with each other, and instructs the partners to designate one member of each dyad to be the leader and the other to be the follower.

IV. Each leader receives a blindfold. The leaders are instructed to take the followers to the entrance of the room in which the maze is set up and to blindfold the followers just prior to entering the room.

V. After the followers have been blindfolded, each leader receives a copy of the Maze Rules Sheet and is instructed to read it silently. While this is being done, the scorekeeper is positioned in the center of the maze. (Five minutes.)

VI. The dyads line up at one end of the maze to begin round 1. Each follower enters the maze and is directed through by his or her leader before the next dyad attempts the task. As each pair begins, the scorekeeper records the leader's name and the time. During each trial, the scorekeeper keeps a record of the number of "hits" (times the follower touches a chair or a wall) and records the time at which the follower leaves the maze. (Approximately two minutes for each dyad.)

VII. When all trials have been completed, round 2 begins, with the followers going in the *opposite direction* through the maze.

VIII. At the conclusion of round 2, the entire group is assembled. The scorekeeper reports on the ranges and averages for times and hits for rounds 1 and 2.

IX. The facilitator leads a general discussion of reactions to the experience. Followers are then asked to comment on their reactions as they heard directions being given to other followers during the task and on factors that helped or hindered the development of trust in the leader. Leaders are asked to comment on differences in their feelings during rounds 1 and 2 and on differences in their sense of responsibility for the outcomes of rounds 1 and 2. (Ten minutes.)

X. The facilitator helps to summarize the reported differences between rounds 1 and 2. (Five minutes.)

XI. The participants are divided into small groups and instructed to generate a list of factors that help or hinder communication flow and the development of trust. (Five to ten minutes.)

XII. One member from each small group reports the group's list to the large group. (Five to ten minutes.)

XIII. The small groups are re-formed, and members discuss applications of their learnings. (Ten minutes.)

Variations

I. More than one scorekeeper can be designated and the scorekeeping tasks distributed when working with even-numbered participant groups.

II. Several pairs of volunteers can be assigned to do the task as presented while the rest of the participants observe the interactions. The facilitator then includes the observers' comments in the debriefing session. The focus of the processing remains on identifying factors that influence the development of trust between a leader and a follower working on a joint task.

III. Roles can be reversed for round 2.

IV. If meeting space is limited, a "maze" can be prepared on a sheet of paper and the task revised so that the blindfolded partner draws a continuous line from start to finish, avoiding obstacles on the paper, by following verbal directions supplied by the leader.

Similar Structured Experiences: *Vol. I:* Structured Experience **4**; *Vol. V:* **159**; *'76 Annual:* **175**.
Suggested Instrument: *Vol. I:* "T-P Leadership Questionnaire."

Notes on the Use of "Maze":

Submitted by Gilles L. Talbot.

MAZE RULES SHEET

Instructions: When you are directed to do so, take your blindfolded follower into the room where the maze is set up. Explain to the follower that chairs are arranged to form a maze and that you will provide verbal directions for getting through it. (The follower's objective is to walk through the maze without touching the walls or running into the chairs in the maze. The follower is to obey your instructions once the maze has been entered.)

Wait until it is your turn before leading your follower to the beginning of the maze. At that time, you are to *remain* at the beginning of the maze and direct your follower through only with your voice. The following rules apply to each round:

1. *Round 1:* You may say anything you like to the follower, but the follower may *not* speak to you. *Tell your follower this rule at the beginning of round 1.*
2. *Round 2:* You and the follower may converse freely while the follower is in the maze, i.e., the follower may ask questions or ask for clarification of your directions. Tell your follower this rule at the beginning of round 2. Direct your follower through the maze from the *opposite direction* (i.e., enter at the exit for round 1) during round 2.

The scorekeeper will record your starting time, the number of times your follower "hits" (touches a wall or a chair in the maze), and the time at which your follower leaves the maze.

MAZE SCORE SHEET

Name of Leader	Round 1		Round 2	
	Hits	Time	Hits	Time
1.				
2.				
3.				
4.				
5.				
6.				
7.				
8.				
9.				
10.	h_1	t_1	h_2	t_2
Totals:				
Divide by the number of dyads:				
Averages:				

RESULTS:

avg. $h_1 > h_2$

$t_1 > t_2$

308. STRUCTURES: INTERGROUP COMPETITION

Goals

    I. To study the effects of intergroup competition on group processes.

    II. To identify helps and hindrances to task accomplishment.

    III. To demonstrate the impact of effective and ineffective communication processes in task groups.

Group Size

    Three to six groups of five to eight members each.

Time Required

    Approximately two hours.

Materials

    I. A copy of the Structures Task Sheet for each group.

    II. A copy of the Structures Design Sheet for the design group.

    III. A copy of the Structures Communicator Sheet for each group.

    IV. A small set of Tinkertoys® for each group.

    V. Newsprint and a felt-tipped marker.

Physical Setting

    A table for each group, set far enough apart that the groups cannot overhear each other, and a method of screening each team's structure from the others (a baffle, as shown below, can be used). In addition, there must be a separate room or meeting area for the communicators.

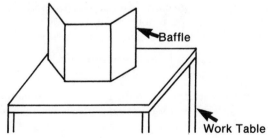

Process

I. The participants are divided into small groups, and the groups are directed to their respective work areas.

II. The facilitator explains to the participants that they will simulate a business operation in which one group will design a prototype structure and will give manufacturing rights to whichever task group is able to accurately reproduce the structure the quickest. The facilitator distributes a copy of the Structures Task Sheet and a set of Tinkertoys to each group and directs the groups to wait for further instructions before handling the materials.

III. The facilitator then designates one group as the design group (this can be done by placing a mark on the bottom of one Tinkertoy box) and gives a copy of the Structures Design Sheet to that group.

IV. The facilitator directs each group to select one member to serve as communicator. Each communicator receives a copy of the Structures Communicator Sheet.

V. The facilitator directs the subgroup members to read their instruction sheets and ensures that everyone understands the roles and tasks. The task process then begins with a ten-minute planning period. During this period the design team is the only team that may begin to assemble a structure. The design team must complete the prototype within the ten minutes.

VI. The facilitator calls for the first meeting of the communicators. The facilitator monitors the timing of all communication sessions by signaling the start and finish of each. There will be three minutes of work time between communication sessions. The design-team communicator is in charge of the communication sessions and follows the procedures outlined on the Structures Communicator Sheet. (Twenty minutes.)

VII. A task group may begin construction of its structure when its communicator returns to the group following the first communication session. Once work has begun, task-group members may continue to work during ensuing communication sessions. As soon as *one* of the task groups has completed a structure, the facilitator stops the action, and the group's structure is compared with the prototype. If all members of the design group accept the task group's product, all construction stops; if not, the construction process continues until one group produces a structure acceptable to all members of the design group.

VIII. The winning group displays its structure. Subgroup members then discuss their reactions to the activity. (Ten minutes.)

IX. Subgroups are directed to discuss how they organized themselves for the task, what types of communication patterns emerged within the group, and the impact of competition on their group processes. (Fifteen minutes.)

X. The facilitator reconvenes the entire group. A representative from each task group gives a summary report on that group's approach to the task. (Ten minutes.)

XI. The facilitator then asks the participants to identify factors that helped the group accomplish its task and those that hindered task accomplishment. These items are listed on newsprint by the facilitator. (Fifteen minutes.)

XII. The facilitator leads a discussion focusing on the role of the communicator in the process. The list of helps and hindrances may be applied to this discussion by identifying the communication skills needed by key communicators. (Ten minutes.)

XIII. Following this general discussion, new subgroups are formed and participants are instructed to develop strategies that could be used by key communicators in task groups in order to be helpful in accomplishing tasks. (Fifteen minutes.)

XIV. Participants are then asked to state how they plan to use their learnings in their back-home situations. (Ten minutes.)

Variations

I. The facilitator can add a two-minute private communication session for each task-group communicator to meet with the design-group communicator.

II. Instead of having the groups choose one communicator, task-group members can be instructed to take turns serving in this capacity.

III. The design group can be limited to a five-minute construction period at the start of the activity.

IV. Members of the design group can take turns serving as the design-group communicator during the communication sessions. Their task is to develop a variety of effective ways to communicate about the design of their group's structure.

V. The design group can decide whether speed, accuracy, or a combination of both criteria are to be considered in determining a winner from among the task groups. These criteria are then communicated to task groups during the communication sessions.

Similar Structured Experiences: *Vol. II:* Structured Experience **33**; *Vol. III:* **54**; *Vol. V:* **160**; '79 *Annual:* **243**.

Submitted by Anthony C. Stein, Stephen C. Iman, and Albert A. Ramos.

Notes on the Use of "Structures":

STRUCTURES TASK SHEET

Task 1. Choose a communicator for your group. This person will meet with the communicator from each of the other groups at various times during this activity. During these meetings the communicator from the design group will relay information necessary for building the structure to the communicators from the task groups.

You may choose more than one communicator, but only one may represent your group at any one communication session.

Task 2. Build a structure that corresponds to the prototype structure produced by the design group. Your communicator will relay descriptions of the product to you after each communication session.

STRUCTURES DESIGN SHEET

Task 1. Choose a communicator for your group. This person will meet with the communicator from each of the other groups at various times during this activity. During these meetings the communicator from the design group will relay information necessary for building the structure to the communicators from the task groups.

You may choose more than one communicator, but only one may represent your group at any one communication session.

Task 2. Design and build a structure utilizing all the parts found in the Tinkertoy box with the exception of the instruction sheet and the box itself.

Task 3. Plan what information your communicator will relay to the communicators from the other teams during each session.

STRUCTURES COMMUNICATOR SHEET

The purpose of the communication sessions is to share information about the prototype structure between the design group and the task groups.

The design-group communicator is in charge of this session. His or her task is to supply requested information and to be helpful to the task-group communicators. The design-group communicator will decide if questions are to come before or after the communication session unless the format is designated on the schedule below.

After each session, the communicators will return to their respective groups.

Schedule of Communication Sessions

Session	Communication Time	Questions by Task-Group Representatives
1	2 minutes	None
2	2 minutes	None
3	2 minutes	Each group representative is allowed one minute to ask questions. This continues until each group representative has had a turn. All representatives may listen to the information shared between the design-group representative and the other task-group representatives.
4	3 minutes	None
5	3 minutes	Two minutes, open discussion
6	3 minutes	Three minutes, open discussion
7	3 minutes	Each representative is allowed one minute to obtain specific information. All other representatives may listen to this exchange.
8	3 minutes	Questions allowed at any time
9	3 minutes	Questions allowed at any time
10	3 minutes	Questions allowed at any time

309. RESISTANCE: A ROLE PLAY

Goals

I. To provide an opportunity to experience the effects of two different approaches[1] to dealing with resistance.

II. To increase awareness of typical responses to attempts to break down resistance.

III. To develop strategies for coping with resistance from others.

Group Size

Five to seven members each.

Time Required

Two to two and one-half hours.

Materials

I. A copy of the Resistance Team Member Role Sheet for each team member.

II. Two copies of the Resistance Rating Sheet for each team member (excluding the two vice presidents) in each group.

III. A copy of the Resistance Role Sheet: Vice President A for the member from each group who will play vice president A.

IV. A copy of the Resistance Role Sheet: Vice President B for the member from each group who will play vice president B.

V. A Resistance Data Analysis Chart (prepared on newsprint by the facilitator).

VI. Newsprint and a felt-tipped marker.

Physical Setting

A room large enough for groups to listen to their vice presidents' presentations without being disturbed by other groups, or a separate room for each group.

---

[1]This structured experience is based on the Gestalt theory of resistance presented by Edwin C. Nevis at the Gestalt Institute of Cleveland.

Process

I. The facilitator discusses the goals of the experience.

II. The facilitator divides the participants into groups of five to seven members each and directs each group to select a member to play vice president A and one to play vice president B.

III. The facilitator distributes Resistance Team Member Role Sheets and two copies of the Rating Sheet to all team members but not to the two persons who will role play the vice presidents in each group. The facilitator gives a copy of the Resistance Role Sheet: Vice President A to each member playing vice president A and a copy of the Resistance Role Sheet: Vice President B to each member playing vice president B.

IV. Group members read over the materials. (Ten minutes.)

V. The facilitator takes the vice presidents aside for a few minutes to coach them on their roles and to clarify any questions they may have. (Five minutes.)

VI. The vice presidents rejoin their groups, and the groups are directed to separate locations.

VII. The facilitator directs each vice president A to try to convince his team of his position for fifteen minutes.

VIII. The facilitator calls time and directs all team members to fill out one copy of the Resistance Rating Sheet, designating A as vice president. (Five minutes.)

IX. Each vice president B then attempts to convince his team to accept his position. (Fifteen minutes.)

X. Each team member fills out the second Resistance Rating Sheet regarding vice president B. (Five minutes.)

XI. Team members debrief the activity, and the members playing the roles of the vice presidents comment on their experiences. (Fifteen minutes.)

XII. Each team then calculates the average score for each question on both rating sheets. The results are entered on the Resistance Data Analysis Chart (prepared on newsprint by the facilitator), and the chart is posted. (Ten minutes.)

XIII. The facilitator leads the total group in discussing and comparing members' reactions to the experience, using the information from the rating sheets as the basis of comparison. The group discusses differences on the Resistance Data Analysis Chart for vice presidents A and B. Consistent differences across groups are identified and the implications of these differences are discussed. (Twenty to twenty-five minutes.)

XIV. Group members reconvene to discuss ways in which they can use their learnings from the experience in back-home situations involving resistance. (Fifteen minutes.)

Variations

I. With large groups, the activity can be conducted by a "presenting group" with other participants serving as observers. Observers focus on identifying the impact of the vice presidents' behavior in attempting to cope with team members' resistance.

II. To shorten the time required for the activity, both vice presidents can attempt to cope with team members simultaneously, thus heightening the differences in their coping styles. Team members then record their reactions to the experience in total.

Similar Structured Experiences: '79 *Annual:* Structured Experiences **234, 238**.

Suggested Instruments: '74 *Annual:* "Interpersonal Communication Inventory"; '76 *Annual:* "Inventory of Anger Communication (IAC)."

Lecturette Sources: '74 *Annual:* "Conflict-Resolution Strategies," "The 'Shouldist' Manager"; '77 *Annual:* "Constructive Conflict in Discussions: Learning to Manage Disagreements Effectively," "Handling Group and Organizational Conflict"; '79 *Annual:* "Transactions in the Change Process," "Encouraging Others to Change Their Behavior."

Notes on the Use of "Resistance":

Submitted by H. B. Karp.

RESISTANCE TEAM MEMBER ROLE SHEET

You are an experienced manager and have been a department head in this company for four years. You take pride in your ability to get things done in your own way, and the company has recognized this with the rapid promotions and pay increases that you have received.

Recently you have been aware of increasing unrest on the part of the younger workers and supervisors in the organization. In your opinion, if other department heads acted more directly and independently with their subordinates, this kind of problem would be minimized.

About ten days ago, you received a memo from the executive vice president, to whom you report, in which he detailed his reactions to an exciting seminar he attended on team building. He has decided that the top level of management should be reorganized and trained to begin functioning as a management team. The memo identified the managers included in this reorganization, and you are one of them.

You are not happy about this designation since you are not, and never have been, a believer in the team approach. You think that team building is a waste of time and is just a way for ineffective managers to cover up their incompetence and avoid taking responsibility for their own mistakes. You have friends in other organizations who work this way and they report problems with it. You know that it will take a lot of extra time and effort to set this team business in motion. Besides, you do not feel comfortable in suggesting things to other managers in their areas of expertise, and you do not want some outsider telling you how to run your department. Furthermore, you do not like, respect, or trust some of the others who will be on the team and would prefer not to work closely with them.

The vice president has scheduled the first meeting with the team in ten minutes. You plan to deal with this issue at the outset.

RESISTANCE RATING SHEET

Vice President   A   B
(Circle the appropriate letter)

Having just left the first meeting of the new management team, please indicate your impressions of the team and the vice president on the sheet below:

1. To what extent do you trust the vice president as your team's leader?

1	2	3	4	5	6	7
Not at all						To a great extent

2. How do you feel now about working with the other team members?

1	2	3	4	5	6	7
Uncooperative						Cooperative

3. To what extent, if any, has your attitude toward team building changed?

1	2	3	4	5	6	7
More resistant						More receptive

4. How willing are you to give the team approach a chance—say for six months?

1	2	3	4	5	6	7
Totally resistant						Very willing

RESISTANCE ROLE SHEET: VICE PRESIDENT A

You recently have been promoted to executive vice president for internal affairs of a large company. For some time you have felt that management team building throughout the entire organization would produce tremendous results. You recently attended a seminar on team building and are convinced that the sooner a move is made in this direction, the better.

As you see it, the main advantages of team building are:

1. Work can be divided to take advantage of the different skills of the team members.
2. It will provide a support system for managers, who are currently isolated in their own departments.
3. Managers will stimulate each other's thinking, thus becoming more creative.
4. It will create the flexibility that is needed to deal with a variety of problems.
5. It will provide the base for project management, should that be indicated.
6. In other companies that you know of, it has led to significant changes in corporate policy that were not otherwise easy to achieve.

You have informed the management team of your intention and today you are going to meet the managers for the first time as a team. You have a lot riding on this move, not only in terms of what is best for the company but also because this is your first major decision in your new position. You have heard through the grapevine that there is a good bit of grumbling about this change. Your managers are sharp, effective people, but they are used to working almost totally independently. You expect to meet some stiff resistance at this meeting.

Your Approach to the Team's Resistance
You are to do your best to influence as many team members as you can to accept the concept of team building. Your goal is to break down or work around the resistance that the managers will offer.

In addition to making points that appeal to professional pride, feel free to influence the managers with:

1. facts and figures
2. an appeal to loyalty and fair play
3. your own power and status
4. guilt
5. self-interests and benefits.

Use any other methods that fit for *you*. Keep in mind that it would be very helpful to get most if not all of the managers "on board" at this meeting, since this is the most prestigious group in the company. If you can get them to join you, it will influence others who are ambivalent or negative to the approach.

RESISTANCE ROLE SHEET: VICE PRESIDENT B

You recently have been promoted to executive vice president for internal affairs of a large company. For some time you have felt that management team building throughout the entire organization would produce tremendous results. You recently attended a seminar on team building and are convinced that the sooner a move is made in this direction, the better.

As you see it, the main advantages of team building are:

1. Work can be divided to take advantage of the different skills of the team members.
2. It will provide a support system for managers, who are currently isolated in their own departments.
3. Managers will stimulate each other's thinking, thus becoming more creative.
4. It will create the flexibility that is needed to deal with a variety of problems.
5. It will provide the base for project management, should that be indicated.
6. In other companies that you know of, it has led to significant changes in corporate policy that were not otherwise easy to achieve.

You have informed the management team of your intention and today you are going to meet the managers for the first time as a team. You have a lot riding on this move, not only in terms of what is best for the company but also because this is your first major decision in your new position. You have heard through the grapevine that there is a good bit of grumbling about this change. Your managers are sharp, effective people, but they are used to working almost totally independently. You expect to meet some stiff resistance at this meeting.

Your Approach to the Team's Resistance
Your main aim for this session is to help the managers to express all their reservations. Try to elicit the most frank statements you can from each manager.

Give arguments in favor of team building only when the managers directly and specifically ask for them. Furthermore, do not talk about any future action steps until you are convinced that the managers have expressed all of their objections and negative feelings.

While it would be very nice if you could get agreement and clear support in this first meeting, you realize that the likelihood of that happening is rather small. If the resistance you anticipate cannot honestly be reduced to a workable level, you are much better off leaving things as they are for now. The very last thing you want or need is a lot of "yes sirs" now and no support once you have made the changes. So, while you maintain your opinion, you realize that it is better not to force the issue.

RESISTANCE DATA ANALYSIS CHART

Question	Vice President	Group 1	Group 2	Group 3
1	A			
	B			
	Change			
2	A			
	B			
	Change			
3	A			
	B			
	Change			
4	A			
	B			
	Change			
5	A			
	B			
	Change			

310. ORGANIZATIONAL TA: INTERPERSONAL COMMUNICATION

Goals

I. To gain insight into the effects on communication of the three ego states: parent (P), adult (A), and child (C).

II. To have the experience of operating from each of these three ego states in confrontation situations.

III. To acquire skills in observing interactions based on these three ego states.

IV. To explore the benefits of operating from an adult ego state in confrontation situations.

Group Size

Four members each.

Time Required

Approximately two hours.

Materials

I. A copy of the Organizational TA Sample Behaviors Sheet for each participant.

II. A copy of the appropriate Organizational TA Role Sheet for each of the four role players in each group.

III. A copy of the Organizational TA Observer Sheet for each participant.

IV. Newsprint and a felt-tipped marker.

Physical Setting

Enough space so that each group can role play without disturbing the other groups.

Process

I. The facilitator introduces the activity as one that explores various ways in which people confront each other in organizations and gives a brief lecturette on Transactional Analysis. (Fifteen minutes.)

II. The facilitator distributes a copy of the Organizational TA Sample Behaviors Sheet to each participant and has members of the group practice by taking turns reading the statements, with appropriate vocal expression, until all statements have been read aloud. The facilitator uses this opportunity to coach participants and to re-emphasize the points made during the lecturette. (Ten minutes.)

III. The facilitator divides the participants into groups of four members each. Each group of four further subdivides into two dyads, designated as Pair A and Pair B.

IV. The facilitator instructs the members that there will be four different role-play situations and four different interactions within each situation, and that each role player will have a chance to practice interacting from the TA ego states of child, parent, and adult during these role plays. In situations one and three, Pair A will role play and Pair B will observe. In situations two and four, Pair B will role play and Pair A will observe.

V. The facilitator distributes a copy of the Organizational TA Observer Sheet to each participant and reads the instructions aloud.

VI. The facilitator then distributes to Pair A a copy of the Organizational TA Role Sheet—Situation One and to Pair B a copy of the Organizational TA Role Sheet—Situation Two. The partners are directed to read the situations silently and decide who is to be role player one and who is to be role player two prior to starting each situation. They are not to show their role sheets to each other.

VII. The facilitator announces the beginning of Situation One, Interaction One, and instructs each Pair A to role play while the related Pair B observes. After two minutes, the facilitator directs the role players to continue in the TA ego states indicated for Interaction Two. After another two minutes, he directs them to switch to Interaction Three, and so on. After all interactions have been role played (eight to ten minutes), the facilitator calls time and directs the role players to tell each other and the observers what TA ego states they were playing during each interaction. They are not to show their role sheets to each other.

VIII. The facilitator announces the beginning of Situation Two and instructs that each Pair B role play while the Pair As serve as observers. Each of the four interactions is completed, in turn, as in step VII.

IX. After Situation Two is completed, the facilitator remarks that each situation ends with an adult-adult interaction. He then rereads aloud the description of adult behavior from the Organizational TA Sample Behaviors Sheet and remarks that the adult is a problem-solving person. The facilitator then encourages the groups *not* to refer to the sample behaviors during the remaining interactions. The facilitator also allows a longer period of time for the adult-adult interactions.

X. Situations Three and Four are then distributed to the appropriate pairs, read, and role played. (Twenty minutes.)

XI. The four members of each group discuss: their feelings about playing the different TA roles; their reactions to the other person who was operating from a different TA ego state; and awarenesses they had about themselves during the role-play situations. (Ten minutes.)

XII. The total group is reassembled, and the members discuss the following questions:
1. What are the consequences of child-parent or parent-child interactions?
2. What are the consequences of adult-adult interactions?
3. What helps or hinders us from engaging in adult-adult interactions in many confrontation situations?

The facilitator posts the answers generated from question 3. (Fifteen minutes.)

XIII. The facilitator instructs group members to select a partner and to generate strategies for dealing with back-home situations on an adult-adult level by applying the content on the group lists. (Ten minutes.)

Variations

I. Partners can be formed instead of groups of four. These two can role play all interactions and give each other feedback. Groups of three can be formed and divided into one observer and two role players who rotate roles for each of the four situations.

II. Participants can role play the ego state that most readily comes to mind during their interactions in the situations.

III. The role plays can be allowed to develop during the time allotted without the facilitator signaling the stop and start of the four interactions within each situation.

IV. The content of the role plays can be revised so as to represent more typical situations.

Lecturette Sources: '73 *Annual:* "Confrontation: Types, Conditions, and Outcomes," "A Transactional Analysis Primer"; '74 *Annual:* "Conflict-Resolution Strategies."

Submitted by Rich Strand and Frederic R. Wickert.

Notes on the Use of "Organizational TA":

ORGANIZATIONAL TA SAMPLE BEHAVIORS SHEET

Child
Confronter
1. I want my . . . (demanding)
2. This is no fair . . . (complaining)
3. Aw, come on . . . (complaining)
4. I know you're right, but . . . (placating)
5. If you'll do this . . . (bargaining)

Confrontee
1. It's not my fault . . . (pouting)
2. I don't know what to do . . . (confused)
3. No, I won't do it . . . (angry)
4. O.K., O.K., I'll do it . . . (avoiding)

Parent
Confronter
1. What is going on here? . . . (angry)
2. You'll have to solve my problem right away . . . (demanding)
3. I knew it, I just knew it . . . (condescending)
4. You better do something, or I'll . . . (threatening)

Confrontee
1. You are responsible for it . . . (blaming)
2. You should do it . . . (controlling)
3. Don't get upset; it's nothing . . . (avoiding)
4. Things could be worse . . . (avoiding)

Adult
Confronter
1. We have a problem. Let's see if . . . (problem solving)
2. Let me tell you my problem . . . (information giving)
3. I understand that you can help me . . . (checking)
4. I feel upset. I just found out . . . (disclosing)

Confrontee
1. Let's see if we can solve your problem . . . (problem solving)
2. Can you tell me more . . . (information seeking)
3. Let me see if I understand you . . . (checking)
4. I think I understand how you feel . . . (defusing)

Structured Experience   310

ORGANIZATIONAL TA ROLE SHEETS

(Roles should be cut apart and distributed separately to appropriate role players.)

Role Player One—Pair A

Situation One: Passenger

Interaction 1: child

Interaction 2: parent

Interaction 3: child

Interaction 4: adult

You just flew into the airport and went to pick up your luggage at the baggage pick-up area. All the other passengers from your flight found their baggage, but yours was not there. You were told to go to the lost-baggage desk and have just arrived there.

Role Player Two—Pair A

Situation One: Airline Employee

Interaction 1: parent

Interaction 2: child

Interaction 3: adult

Interaction 4: adult

You are in charge of the lost-baggage desk at the airport. Until about the last half-hour, the day has been really hectic. You just looked up from your paperwork to see someone approaching your desk. This is probably another passenger with lost luggage.

Role Player One—Pair B

Situation Two: Employee

Interaction 1: parent

Interaction 2: child

Interaction 3: adult

Interaction 4: adult

You have just found out at work that you have been rescheduled to take your vacation at a time when you have all sorts of reasons to stay in town. You have already made reservations for what you were once told was your vacation time and you don't want to change them. You are going in to confront your boss.

Role Player Two—Pair B

Situation Two: Boss

Interaction 1: child

Interaction 2: parent

Interaction 3: parent

Interaction 4: adult

Among all the other things you have to do is the allocation and distribution of the annual vacation schedule for your group of twenty-one subordinates. It is a real headache to plan the schedule so that the employees can take their summer vacations at the times they asked for and still keep operations going. (Your company operates all summer and does not have an annual vacation shutdown.) In fact, when it came to the last slots in the schedule, you had to put a few newer employees down for times they may not like very well, but there was no other way you could make the schedule work out. Just now you looked up to see one of these employees coming toward your desk. This person does not look happy.

....

Role Player Two—Pair A

Situation Three: Supervisor

    Interaction 1: parent

    Interaction 2: parent

    Interaction 3: adult

    Interaction 4: adult

You are in charge of five employees. Pat is fairly new and a bit independent, but, as you have observed, is a hard worker. During this last week, however, Pat has been about an hour late twice. Today it was an hour and a half. You have just called Pat into your office.

....

Role Player One—Pair A

Situation Three: Pat

    Interaction 1: child

    Interaction 2: parent

    Interaction 3: child

    Interaction 4: adult

You are a relatively recent addition to the staff. You like your supervisor, the other members of the staff, and your work. At the same time you like to do things your own way without too much interference from others. Before you took this job, you lived and worked on the other side of town. It has been a pain trying to get across town every morning. You plan to move closer to work eventually. You know that you have not always made it to work on time, but you work more than hard enough to make up for any time you might lose. You have just been called into your supervisor's office. You don't know what it is about.

Role Player Two—Pair B

Situation Four: Manufacturing Manager

Interaction 1: parent

Interaction 2: adult

Interaction 3: parent

Interaction 4: adult

You are in charge of one of several product-line departments of a large computer company. Lately your department has been having a lot of "down time" because of an insufficient supply of plastic casing. You are on your way to see the supply manager about this.

Role Player One—Pair B

Situation Four: Supply Manager

Interaction 1: parent

Interaction 2: child

Interaction 3: adult

Interaction 4: adult

You're in charge of the supply operation for several product-line departments of a large computer company. To supply these departments with the many materials they need is a continuous problem. Purchasing gets behind, major suppliers cannot get materials, and it is one thing after another. You do the best you can. You just looked up to see a manager of one of the product-line departments coming down the aisle toward you.

ORGANIZATIONAL TA OBSERVER SHEET

Instructions: Your task as an observer is to develop skills in differentiating between communications that represent parent, child, and adult ego-state functioning.

1. Try to identify the ego states of the confrontee and confronter. If necessary, make notes to help refresh your memory. Observe body language, choice of words, tone of voice, etc.

2. Check with role players at the end of the role-play situation to see which ego states they depicted.

3. Be prepared to state why you perceived the ego states of the role players as you did.

4. If there is a discrepancy between the reported or intended role-play ego state and your perceptions, *note this* but do not argue with the role player.

5. Be prepared to discuss later the possible consequences of the various interactions (e.g., continued emotional reactions, development of hidden agendas, hidden information, lack of cooperation during problem solving).

311. RISK GAME: COMPETITION AND TEAM BUILDING

Goals

    I. To increase awareness of one's preferred level of risk taking.

    II. To increase awareness of how the attitudes of others can affect one's choices and level of risk taking.

    III. To study the effects of intergroup competition on intragroup communication processes.

Group Size

    Eight to twenty-four participants, in even numbers.

Time Required

    Approximately two hours.

Materials

    I. Eighteen to forty-five copies of the Risk Game Tally Sheet (three copies for each dyad and three additional copies for each pair of teams—refer to Process).

    II. A Risk Game Board for each group (to be prepared on newsprint by the facilitator prior to the experience).

    III. A die for each group.

    IV. A pencil for each group.

    V. A variety of small items (key, pen, lighter, etc.) to be used as markers for each participant.

Physical Setting

    Enough room to allow all groups to position themselves so that each group has a section of wall to throw its die against.

Process

    I. The facilitator introduces the activity by stating the goals. The rules of the Risk Game are prepared ahead and posted on newsprint. A brief overview of the activity is given and the three main points in the rules are emphasized:

1. The participants must keep track of each move because the move number determines the level of risk that can be chosen.
2. The game is over on the twenty-second move, and a draw is declared if no one has reached position 71 on the board.
3. Any member who must retreat more spaces than have been accrued loses the game at that point. For example, if a participant is on position 11 and then rolls a six, under the level-2 risk-condition option, the twelve spaces retreated would put the marker off the board. The game would be over for that dyad at that point. The winner would be the player remaining on the board.

(Ten minutes.)

II. The facilitator says that each participant is to look around the room and pick as an opponent someone he thinks will give him a good game, then join that person in a location along a wall and away from others. (If a participant's invitation to play is refused, the participant is to pick another opponent.)

III. The facilitator distributes three copies of the Risk Game Tally Sheet, a die, and a pencil to each dyad. He may either direct each participant to select an individualized "marker" from among his personal effects or may bring a selection of markers and distribute them to the participants.

IV. Phase 1 of the game is played. (Fifteen minutes.) Several games may be played during this phase of the activity. A new Risk Game Tally Sheet should be used to keep track of the rounds for each game played.

V. An even number of groups ("teams") of four to six members each is formed. Each team chooses a captain, who will roll the die and move the team piece. The team also chooses a recorder, who is charged with keeping notes on the game strategy and keeping track of the rounds completed.

VI. The facilitator instructs each team to choose as an opponent a team that it thinks it can beat. (If a team's challenge is refused, it is to pick another team.) The teams are encouraged to organize themselves so that communication among team members flows smoothly, efficiently, and with satisfaction to the team members.

VII. Each pair of teams receives three copies of the Risk Game Tally Sheet. (A new Risk Game Tally Sheet is used for each game played.) One or more games can be played between teams in the time allotted. (Twenty minutes.)

VIII. At the end of this phase, team members debrief the activity by reviewing their results, the number of games won, etc. (Ten minutes.)

IX. The facilitator then assembles the entire group and leads a discussion of the experience. The following questions can be used to guide the discussion:
1. How did teams approach the game? What strategies did they develop for winning?

2. What contingency strategies did teams develop for when they were behind?
3. What impact did individual members' risk-taking preferences have on the team's risk-level choices?
4. Did individual members' willingness to take risks increase once they became members of a team? If so, what factors influenced them?
5. What communication networks and work patterns developed within the teams?
6. How did patterns change as the teams played more games?

(Twenty minutes.)

X. The teams are then reconvened to discuss members' personal learnings regarding risk taking. The focus of this discussion is to identify factors that influence an individual's willingness to take risks in various situations. (Ten minutes.)

XI. The participants are directed to complete this sentence: "What I learned (or relearned) about taking risks is . . . ." (Five minutes.)

XII. Team members then share their statements and discuss applications of their learnings. (Ten minutes.)

Variations

I. Prior to the activity, the facilitator can present a lecturette on motivation and risk taking and ask the participants to rate themselves as high, medium, or low on two independent measures: need to achieve and fear of failure. During the processing of personal learnings, team members comment on these self-perceptions, based on their observations during game interactions.

II. Some participants can serve as judges or observers.

III. Based on the outcome of the first round, several strategies for team composition can be used:
1. Winners can be grouped as a team against other winners, and the same strategy used with groups of losers. A rank order of best to worst teams can result.
2. Winners can play in teams against teams of losers.
3. Teams can be formed so that they include both winners and losers.

IV. The facilitator can draw attention to the fact that there may be some, all, or no winners. If everyone elects a "no-risk" condition, only half the players are expected to cross the finish line by the twenty-first move. A general discussion of the costs and advantages of risk taking is then conducted.

Game Rules

1. Teams select a game piece (marker).

2. Team captains call a risk level within the constraints of the rules prior to rolling the die. Note: Team captains may call the risk level for rounds 8, 9, 15, 18, and 21 by consulting or not consulting with teammates.

3. The rolled die must hit a wall to ensure a fair roll.

4. The team captain advances or retreats the team's game piece the indicated number of moves on the game board.

5. If the game piece is required to retreat a number of moves *more* than has been already gained on the board, the team loses the game at the moment it becomes overextended. This is the only way the game can be lost.

6. Each round must be marked off on the Risk Game Tally Sheet as it is completed.

7. The game is over at the end of the twenty-first turn. The only way to win the game is to cross the winner's line prior to the end of the twenty-first turn.

Similar Structured Experience: *Vol. II:* Structured Experience **36**.

Lecturette Sources: '72 *Annual:* "Risk-Taking and Error Protection Styles"; '73 *Annual:* "Risk-Taking."

Notes on the Use of "Risk Game":

Submitted by Allen J. Schuh.

RISK GAME TALLY SHEET

Check off as rounds are completed:	Round	Risk Level
_____	1	I
_____	2	I
_____	3	I
_____	4	I
_____	5	I
_____	6	I
_____	7	I
_____	8	*I or II
_____	9	*I or II
_____	10	I or II
_____	11	I or II
_____	12	I or II
_____	13	I or II
_____	14	I or II
_____	15	*I, II, or III
_____	16	I, II, or III
_____	17	I, II, or III
_____	18	*I, II, or III
_____	19	I, II, or III
_____	20	I, II, or III
_____	21	*I, II, or III

*Team captain *may* select risk level by consulting or not consulting with team members.

Explanation of Risk Levels:

   I. (Low risk): Marker advances by the number of spaces indicated on the die.

 II. (Moderate risk):

If die shows	Advance	Retreat
1	2	
2		4
3	6	
4		8
5	10	
6		12

III. (High risk):

If die shows	Advance	Retreat
1	3	
2		6
3	9	
4		12
5	15	
6		18

RISK GAME BOARD

Start

1	28	29	56	57
2	27	30	55	58
3	26	31	54	59
4	25	32	53	60
5	24	33	52	61
6	23	34	51	62
7	22	35	50	63
8	21	36	49	64
9	20	37	48	65
10	19	38	47	66
11	18	39	46	67
12	17	40	45	68
13	16	41	44	69
14	15	42	43	70

Finish

312. VACATION SCHEDULE: GROUP PROBLEM SOLVING

Goals

I. To explore the advantages and disadvantages of using group-decision-making procedures to resolve complex issues.

II. To increase awareness of supervisory responsibilities in decision-making situations.

Group Size

Any number of groups of five members each.

Time Required

Approximately two hours.

Materials

I. A copy of a different Vacation Schedule Role-Play Sheet for each group member (supervisor, Marge, George, Annie, and Sam).

II. Newsprint and a felt-tipped marker for each group.

Physical Setting

A room large enough so that each group can work separately, or a separate room for each group.

Process

I. The facilitator informs the participants that they will be involved in a role-play situation. He says that each person will be supplied with information about his or her character as well as some information about the immediate situation and that, beyond the information supplied, the participants should interpret and act out the roles as they wish.

II. The facilitator divides the participants into groups of five members each. If there are participants left over, the ones who are not assigned roles can act as observers. Each observer is assigned to a specific group.

III. The facilitator directs each group to a separate location, gives each member of each group one of the five different Vacation Schedule Role Sheets, and allows five minutes for the members to read their sheets and prepare for the activity.

IV. The facilitator announces that the groups have thirty minutes in which to complete the activity and tells them to begin.

V. The facilitator calls time and instructs the subgroups to debrief the activity by considering the following points:
1. What solution was reached in each group?
2. Was the supervisor in each group satisfied with the solution? Were the persons playing Marge, George, Annie, and Sam (individually) in each group satisfied with the solution?
3. How was the problem identified by the supervisor?
4. What approach did the supervisor take to solving the problem, e.g., solving it himself, asking the workers to help, telling the workers to solve it?
5. How did the workers feel about the supervisor's approach to the problem?

These points can be posted on newsprint. If subgroups are spread out, a separate sheet should be prepared beforehand for each subgroup. If observers have been used, they report their observations to the group at this time. (Fifteen minutes.)

VI. The facilitator then reassembles all the participants and leads a discussion of the learnings from the experience. The following items can be included:
1. In a situation of this type, what are the advantages and disadvantages of a supervisor's assumption of responsibility for a decision? In what situations should workers be expected to participate in and contribute to the decision-making process?
2. What group decision-making techniques are helpful?
3. What decision-making techniques are not helpful to group decision making?

(Twenty minutes.)

VII. The participants are instructed to generate statements of principles and guidelines for conducting such group-decision-making meetings. These statements are posted on newsprint by the facilitator. (Twenty minutes.)

VIII. Subgroup members are then instructed to reassemble and discuss the application of these guidelines to their back-home settings by identifying situations in which group-decision-making procedures would be appropriate. (Fifteen minutes.)

Variations

I. One group can role play while the remaining participants observe.

II. The supervisor alone can be given role instructions. The other group members can be directed to respond naturally to the situation. Processing can then focus on factors that influenced the group's decision-making processes and group members' behavior during the activity.

Similar Structured Experiences: '77 *Annual:* Structured Experiences **185, 192;** *Vol. VII:* **260.**
Suggested Instrument: '78 *Annual:* "Phases of Integrated Problem Solving (PIPS)."

Notes on the Use of "Vacation Schedule":

Submitted by L. B. Day and Meeky Blizzard. Adapted from American Bankers Association, *Supervisory Training Program,* 1980. Used with permission.

VACATION SCHEDULE ROLE-PLAY SHEET

Supervisor

Background: You supervise twenty people in the accounting department of a major insurance company. Vacation scheduling has always been a problem here because of the increase in activity during the summer months. This year, however, you developed a vacation schedule early, checked with your staff, and by the end of March had a schedule that showed only two people out during any one week. This fit in with your objective of having only two scheduled absences per week.

Next week will be an exception to your policy. Two employees, George and Annie, were already scheduled to take their vacations when another employee, Sam, transferred into your area on the condition that he could take his vacation next week as previously scheduled. Since George had already planned to take his family camping in Idaho, Annie was going to Hawaii for her annual family reunion, and you were eager to have Sam join your staff, you decided that things would be all right, as long as nothing else came up.

1:15 P.M. Just as you were returning from lunch, Marge approached your desk with a problem. Her husband, who has been out of work for several months, has just landed a week-long job hauling goods from the next state, beginning Monday. The difficulty is that he needs her to go with him because she is the only one who knows his business operation well enough to help him on such short notice. She has not taken her vacation yet, and you know from previous conversations how important this hauling job is to their financial stability. But if Marge were gone next week, four people would be out—hardly an ideal situation for the rest of the staff.

After wrestling with the problem, you told Marge that she could take next week off. You felt that you had made a good decision; Marge always does more than her share of the work.

1:30 P.M. You received a call from Mike's wife. Mike has been out the last two days with a bad cold, but now his wife says he is scheduled for a tonsillectomy Monday and will not be in next week at all. This raises the number of people out next week to five!

1:45 P.M. As you reconsidered the wisdom of letting Marge take next week off, Bryan strolled up to your desk. He had a job interview during his lunch hour and will be starting his new job *Monday*. Now you will be *six* people short next week; you shudder to think of the chaos that will result.

You are not sure how you are going to solve this problem. Can your department realistically manage next week with six people gone? If not, what are the alternatives? Should you handle this situation alone or involve others?

2:00 P.M. You have just called a meeting with George, Annie, Marge, and Sam to discuss the problem. Mike and Bryan, of course, are out of the schedule altogether. You have asked the workers to meet with you in the conference room.

Structured Experience 312

VACATION SCHEDULE ROLE-PLAY SHEET

Marge

Background: It is about two o'clock on a Friday afternoon in late June. Your husband, Joe, who has not been able to locate any work for the past few months, called about an hour ago with the news that he has a week-long contract to haul goods from the next state beginning Monday, but he needs you to go along with him to handle the bookkeeping and other functions. You are not scheduled to take your vacation until August. You talked to your supervisor about the situation, and your supervisor agreed to reschedule your vacation for next week.

You were elated when Joe called with the good news about the job next week. Not only have things been pretty tight financially these past few months, but this period of unemployment has really been a drain on Joe's usually optimistic outlook. Now he has a chance to earn some money, regain his self-esteem, and maybe even continue to work with this distributor. You were a bit concerned when you learned that he needed you to go with him on this run, since you know how much your absence will increase the work load in the department, and you do not want to be a burden to your friends here. But, in your mind, it is a valid, unavoidable emergency, since you are the only one who knows Joe's business well enough to help him out on such short notice.

Your supervisor understands the situation and has been a real friend during the crisis of the last few months, providing financial counseling as well as moral support. To show your appreciation, you are planning to put in a couple of hours of overtime before you leave tonight, to reduce the work load a bit.

The Setting: Your supervisor has just called a brief meeting in the conference room "to talk about a problem in next week's schedule."

VACATION SCHEDULE ROLE-PLAY SHEET

George

Background: It is about two o'clock on a Friday afternoon in late June—the last day of work before your vacation, which you scheduled with your supervisor in February. You, your wife, and two children (ages eight and nine) are leaving early tomorrow morning to go camping in Idaho.

The thought of your vacation next week is just about the only thing that has kept you going all week. It has been pretty hectic here, and your morale is badly in need of that rejuvenating mountain air. It seems like years since you have spent a relaxed moment with your family, and beginning early tomorrow morning the four of you will have nine days to explore the Idaho wilderness together. You were just thinking about how excited the kids were last night as you made some last-minute plans. The thought made you smile before you turned back to the mound of paperwork left do do before five o'clock.

The Setting: Your supervisor has just called a brief meeting in the conference room "to talk about a problem in next week's schedule."

VACATION SCHEDULE ROLE-PLAY SHEET

Annie

Background: It is about two o'clock on a Friday afternoon in late June—your last day of work before vacation, which you scheduled with your supervisor in February. You are leaving for Hawaii this evening, to attend your seventh annual family reunion.

There are only six more hours before your plane leaves for the islands, and you can hardly wait. Years ago, when your family started this annual get-together, you looked at it as an obligation and a chore—except that it was a chance to go to Hawaii again. Now, however, your perspective has changed and you really look forward to seeing everyone again—even your brother Sam, who is quite a bore until you get to know him. And this year the reunion will be special because your sister and her family will be there after spending three years in Sweden. You hope her superb wit has not changed; it has been such a long time since the two of you have had a good laugh together.

You just hope that things will not be as busy at work when you get back. The recent work load has been unreal!

The Setting: Your supervisor has just called a brief meeting in the conference room "to talk about a problem in next week's schedule."

VACATION SCHEDULE ROLE-PLAY SHEET

Sam

Background: It is about two o'clock on a Friday afternoon in late June. You are the newest employee in this work group, having joined the department a month ago. Your vacation, due to begin Monday morning, was originally scheduled with your old supervisor in March. When you applied for this position, you were told that you could keep the same vacation week although it would stretch the normal policy a bit. You plan to spend your vacation at a nearby lake with some friends. You are looking forward to it.

You were told that this new job would be a challenge, and nobody was kidding you! You thought that after a month in this department you would be feeling at least somewhat knowledgeable about your new job, but sometimes trying to learn everything at once is overwhelming. You sure need a break, or maybe even a transfer back to your old area, where you were the resident expert. Although it was boring sometimes, right now you would gladly trade some boredom for a lot of frustration. On the other hand, your new supervisor was really pleased to have someone with your background here and indicated that there was a lot of room for advancement.

You have decided to spend some time during your next week at the lake to think about what you want to do.

The Setting: Your supervisor has just called a brief meeting in the conference room "to talk about a problem in next week's schedule."

313. TANGRAM[1]: LEADERSHIP DIMENSIONS

Goals

    I. To identify key functions of a task-team leader.

    II. To examine the process of leading a team toward the accomplishment of a task.

    III. To experience the information-sharing process within a task team.

    IV. To provide an opportunity to observe the effects of communication processes on members of a task team.

Group Size

Eight to fifteen members.

Time Required

Approximately two hours.

Materials

    I. A large envelope for each team leader, containing:
      1. One copy of the Tangram Leader Instruction Sheet
      2. Three separate Tangram Patterns (I, II and III)[2]
      3. Four plastic bags containing Tangram pieces (to be assembled by the facilitator according to the Directions for Assembling Tangram Pieces)
      4. Masking tape.

    II. A copy of the Tangram Observer Sheet for each observer.

    III. A copy of the Tangram Key Sheet for each participant.

    IV. A pencil for each observer.

    V. Newsprint and a felt-tipped marker.

---

[1]The Tangram is a classic Chinese puzzle.

[2]The Tangram Patterns should be exactly equal in size to the actual Tangram to be constructed.

Physical Setting

A room with furniture arranged in a group-on-group (fishbowl) design. At the center is a large table, five or six chairs, and a newsprint pad. Chairs for the observers are arranged outside the team area, in a circle, at a distance of approximately four feet.

Process

I. The facilitator gives a brief, experiential lecturette on leadership functions, e.g., setting the overall goal, stating specific objectives, planning, communicating, directing, coordinating, and controlling, by eliciting comments from the group members. The functions identified by the group are posted and added to by the facilitator as necessary to represent key aspects of the role requirement. (Fifteen minutes.)

II. The facilitator explains that an experiment will be conducted to explore the group's suggestions. He avoids any mention of the nature of the task.

III. Five or six members are selected to act as the "experimental team"; they are directed to select one of their members to serve as team leader for the rest of the experience.

IV. The facilitator directs the team to its work area and gives the team leader a sealed envelope containing:
   1. One copy of the Tangram Leader Instruction Sheet
   2. Three separate Tangram Patterns (I, II, and III)
   3. *Four* plastic bags containing Tangram pieces
   4. Masking tape.

   The leader is informed that the envelope is not to be opened until the facilitator directs that it be done.

V. The facilitator gives a copy of the Tangram Observer Sheet and a pencil to all remaining participants, tells them that they will observe the team's process, and instructs them to take notes and be ready to discuss their observations after the completion of the experiment. The observers are then directed to sit in the chairs surrounding the team work area.

VI. While the observers are reviewing their instruction sheets, the facilitator directs the team leader to unseal the envelope and to read the instructions silently.

VII. When all participants are ready, the facilitator signals the start of the experiment. During the assembling process, the facilitator acts as the "boss" of the team leader and does not communicate directly with any of the team members. All communication is through the team leader. If the team leader requests more instructions, the facilitator answers that all necessary instructions are on the Tangram Leader Instruction Sheet.

VIII. The facilitator gives the number 14 Tangram piece to the team leader when (and *only if*) the team leader requests it.

IX. When the team leader declares the experiment completed (whether it is successful or not), or at the end of fifteen minutes, the facilitator distributes the Tangram Key Sheet to everyone. He announces that the completed pieces depict an old Chinese person blowing at a candle.

X. The facilitator convenes the observers and instructs them to report their observations of the experimental team's process. (Ten minutes.)

XI. The facilitator instructs the experimental team members to share their reactions to their process by focusing on both leader and member behavior during the task. The facilitator provides guidelines for these discussions by posting a pre-prepared list of typical task-group phenomena:

1. What difficulties did the leader experience in fulfilling his or her linking-pin role in the communication process between the members and the facilitator?
2. How did the leader establish the task to be accomplished; when was this done?
3. When and how did the leader consult with members regarding their individual skills, task resources, or possible contributions?
4. How did the leader's style vary as problems arose or accumulated? How did this affect coordination and direction?
5. How did group members' behavior vary during the task?
6. What additional restrictive norms (not imposed by the task instructions or by the leader) were introduced by group members? How did this affect the team's functioning?

(Twenty minutes.)

XII. The facilitator calls for a report from the group, summarizing the key observations of its members. (Ten minutes.)

XIII. Key ideas related to leadership functions are listed on newsprint. The facilitator then conducts a discussion of the main points on this list and facilitates the members in relating their observations to the pre-experiment list of leadership dimensions created by the group. (Fifteen minutes.)

XIV. The group members discuss applications of these learnings to real-life situations in which they play leadership roles. (Fifteen minutes.)

Variations

I. Several experimental teams with observers can attempt the task simultaneously, with the facilitator available to team leaders on request.

II. Observers can be omitted from the design, and all participants can be placed on experimental teams.

III. Team members can have a pre-task planning session to discuss relevant leader/member behavior for task teams.

IV. Time limits can be stated prior to the start of the task to add the element of time pressure.

V. The time limit can be eliminated from the activity.

VI. The facilitator can call a stop action midway through the task to allow task-team members to review their performance and plan for more effective communication.

Similar Structured Experiences: *Vol. V:* Structured Experiences **159, 162**.

Suggested Instruments: *Vol. I:* "T-P Leadership Questionnaire"; '76 *Annual:* "Leader Effectiveness and Adaptability Description (LEAD)."

Lecturette Sources: '76 *Annual:* "Leadership as Persuasion and Adaptation"; '77 *Annual:* "A Practical Leadership Paradigm."

Notes on the Use of "Tangram":

Submitted by Eduardo Casais.

TANGRAM LEADER INSTRUCTION SHEET

The task:

1. Your team is to construct on the table, with the Tangram pieces herewith, three Tangram figures according to the patterns enclosed, in the following order:

Fig. 1	Fig. 2	Fig. 3

2. Post the Tangram Patterns on newsprint immediately (tape is available for this purpose), so that each member can see them clearly.

3. The task should be accomplished as quickly and as precisely as possible.

Your Role:

1. You are to get the work done through other people. Have your team members do the construction. Do not intervene personally in the physical operation.

2. Distribute the bags containing the Tangram pieces to the respective team members.

3. Explain to your team members which jobs they are to accomplish.

4. Direct and control the team's work during the process, as you think appropriate.

5. All communication from or to the facilitator (who acts as your "boss" during the activity) will be channeled through you.

6. It is your job to announce when the task is completed.

TANGRAM PATTERN I

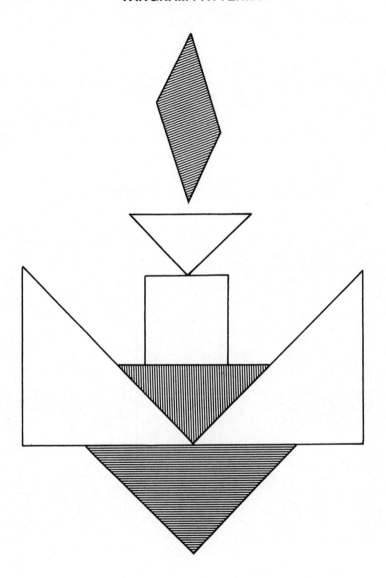

TANGRAM PATTERN II

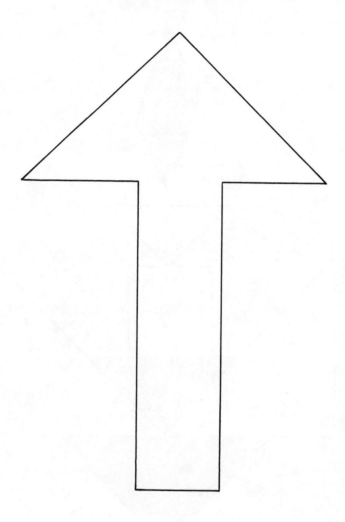

TANGRAM PATTERN III

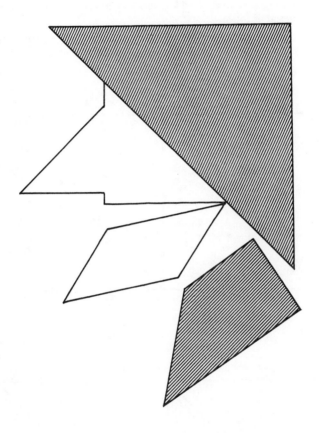

DIRECTIONS FOR ASSEMBLING TANGRAM PIECES

Instructions to the facilitator:

1. Prepare Tangram pieces (numbered for clarity of distribution) by cutting plastic or cardboard material as follows.

   a. *Two rectangles* of equal size, one *white*, the other *colored*, cut into seven pieces, as indicated:

White:

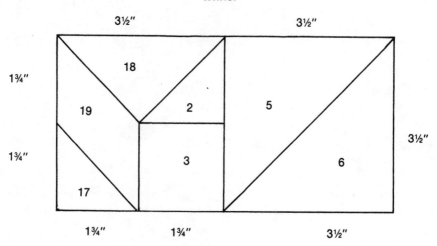

Colored:

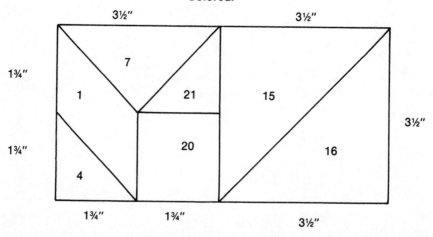

b. *One rectangle,* slightly smaller, *white,* similarly cut into seven pieces:

White:

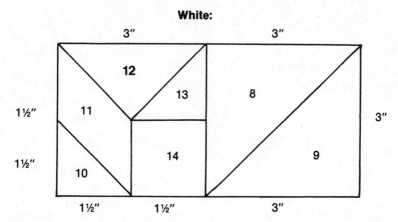

2. Separate the pieces into five sets, slip the first four sets into plastic bags, and mark the bags as follows:

   Team leader (Pieces 5, 6, 15, 16)
   Team member 1 (Pieces 1, 2, 4, 12, 21)
   Team member 2 (Pieces 8, 9, 10, 13, 19, 20)
   Team member 3 (Pieces 3, 7, 11, 17, 18)

   (The remaining piece, 14, is retained by the facilitator until the team leader asks for it.)

3. In a large envelope put the following:
   a. The *four* plastic bags containing the twenty Tangram pieces for the experimental team
   b. The Tangram Leader Instruction Sheet
   c. The three Tangram Patterns (these should be exactly equal in size to the actual Tangram fully constructed).

4. Seal the envelope.

TANGRAM OBSERVER SHEET

Instructions: Observe the experimental team's performance carefully. Note significant events pertaining to the formulation of the task and the team's objectives, the sharing and flow of information, and the leadership performance of the team leader. You may wish to consider the following points:

1. How does the team leader present the goal to the team members?

2. Does the team take its time to fully consider and plan the task, or do the members start before setting rules and procedures?

3. How does the team set objectives? (There are three specific objectives listed on the leader's instruction sheet. No specific time limit has been imposed on the team.) Time will be called at the end of fifteen minutes if the team leader has not signaled that the task has been accomplished before that time.

4. How is the division of the work accomplished?

5. How does the team leader process the information flow? Does he or she communicate with the facilitator effectively?

6. Do all team members participate actively?

7. Does the leader's style of interaction vary during the course of the task? If so, how?

8. Do the team members' styles of interaction vary? If so, how?

Note: You may *not* communicate, either verbally or nonverbally, with the team members during this experiment.

TANGRAM KEY SHEET

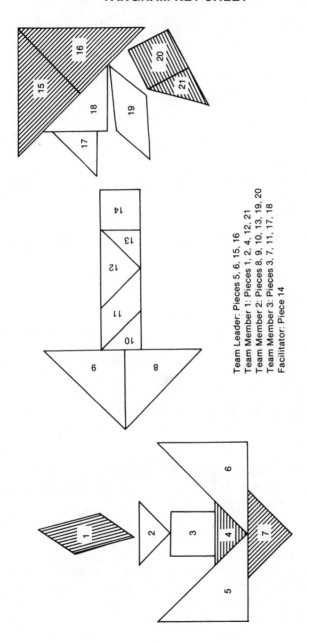

Team Leader: Pieces 5, 6, 15, 16
Team Member 1: Pieces 1, 2, 4, 12, 21
Team Member 2: Pieces 8, 9, 10, 13, 19, 20
Team Member 3: Pieces 3, 7, 11, 17, 18
Facilitator: Piece 14

314. TERRITORY: INTERGROUP NEGOTIATION

Goals

I. To experience the effects of a negotiation activity.

II. To increase awareness of various negotiation strategies.

III. To practice collaboration strategies in intergroup problem solving.

Group Size

Three to six groups of four to six members each.

Time Required

Approximately two and one-half hours.

Materials

I. A copy of the Territory Instruction Sheet for each participant.

II. Two copies of the Territory Terrain Sheet for each group. (This sheet is a map of the room or area that is to be divided by the teams. It should be prepared by the facilitator prior to the activity.)

III. A pencil for each participant.

IV. A roll of crepe-paper streamer in a different color for each group.

V. A roll of masking tape for each group.

Physical Setting

A room that will accommodate all members in planning or discussion, and an empty room or a designated area within the general meeting room that is substantially larger than is needed to physically accommodate the group.

Process

I. The facilitator forms teams in a manner deemed appropriate to the participant group involved, e.g., counting off, having the participants choose teammates, or assignment based on desired sex ratio or other factor.

II. The facilitator distributes one copy of the Territory Instruction Sheet and a pencil to each participant and two copies of the Territory Terrain Sheet to each group. The facilitator reads the Territory Instruction Sheet aloud and then supplies the following verbal instructions:

1. Each team is to meet independently.
2. The team members have twenty minutes (a) to decide how much of the space in the designated territory they want to claim for their team, (b) to develop a plan for getting the space, and (c) to decide on their negotiating strategies.
3. The staking-out activity in round 1 is to be carried out *nonverbally* by the team representatives, working simultaneously.
4. The spaces claimed during round 1 must correspond to the plan submitted by the team.
5. The elected team representative has the authority to negotiate space and alter boundaries on behalf of the group.
6. New representatives may not be elected once the activity has begun.
7. All team representatives must agree on final space allocations by the end of six rounds of negotiation or all space is forfeited.
8. The winning team will be the team with the most physical space at the end of round 6.

III. The teams are directed to depict the configuration of the space they want to claim on the Territory Terrain Sheets and to select one representative to serve as negotiator for the group.

IV. After twenty minutes, or when each team has submitted a copy of its plan to the facilitator, the start of round 1 is announced. The representative from each team is given a roll of crepe paper (each team receives a different color) and a roll of masking tape and is sent to the room or area in which the territory is to be divided. Using the roll of crepe paper (and the team's copy of the Territory Terrain Sheet as a guide) each representative stakes out the space claimed by his team. The facilitator monitors this phase of the activity to ensure that the activity is carried out nonverbally and that no changes are made during this round. The other team members remain in the team meeting area while their representatives carry out the claim-staking task. (Five minutes.)

V. The facilitator calls time and directs round 2, the team-strategy caucus, to begin. (Ten minutes.)

VI. The facilitator monitors each of the remaining rounds, calls time, and reiterates the directions for the next round before it begins.

VII. At the close of round 6, the facilitator declares a winning team, based on criteria established at the start of the activity.

VIII. Group members are instructed to remain in their meeting areas to discuss their general reactions to the activity and to review the strategies used by their negotiators. The strengths and weaknesses of various negotiating styles and strategies employed by the other teams, especially the winning team, are also discussed. (Fifteen minutes.)

IX. The facilitator reassembles the large group, and the teams report on the results of their discussions. (Five minutes.)

X. The facilitator develops a list of the strategies used, summarizing the reported strengths and weaknesses by focusing on key words and ideas. The facilitator then gives a brief lecturette on negotiation strategies, using the list previously generated by the group as a starting point and adding to it when necessary. (Fifteen minutes.)

XI. The participants identify general themes that have emerged during the reporting and listing processes. (Five minutes.)

XII. The teams reconvene to discuss the application of their learnings to back-home negotiation situations. (Ten minutes.)

Variations

I. Team members can accompany their representatives to the territory to be claimed and serve as observers and coaches between each of the rounds of claim staking.

II. A second planning session can be held between rounds 4 and 5 to develop negotiation strategies.

III. New team representatives can be elected after round 2 has been completed.

IV. Other criteria can be used to determine the winning team, e.g., the team closest to its original plan, self-evaluation, or nomination of the winner. The basis for winning can be determined by the facilitator or can be decided by participants through a simple decision-making procedure. However, it is important not to detract from the negotiation focus of the activity by using a complex decision-making procedure at this point.

Similar Structured Experiences: *Vol. II:* Structured Experience **35**; *Vol. III:* **61**; *'72 Annual:* **83**; *'75 Annual:* **147**; *'76 Annual:* **179**; *'77 Annual:* **189**; *Vol. VII:* **263, 265**; *'80 Annual:* **280**.

Suggested Instruments: *'75 Annual:* "Decision-Style Inventory"; *'78 Annual:* "Phases of Integrated Problem Solving (PIPS)."

Lecturette Source: '73 *Annual:* "Win/Lose Situations."

Notes on the Use of "Territory":

Submitted by Phyliss Cooke and Anthony J. Reilly.

TERRITORY INSTRUCTION SHEET

This activity will be conducted in six rounds.

Each team is to depict the amount of space it will claim on the two copies of the Territory Terrain Sheet provided. One copy of this plan is to be given to the facilitator prior to round 1.

The rounds will be conducted as follows:

Round 1 (Five minutes): An elected representative of your team will stake out the space claimed by the team by outlining it with the colored paper streamer supplied to your team. This will be done nonverbally, with representatives from all groups working simultaneously. Representatives will return to their team meeting areas to report on their results as soon as their tasks are completed.

Round 2 (Ten minutes): Team members will caucus to discuss the results of the staking-out activity and their strategy for round 3.

Round 3 (Fifteen minutes): Group representatives will return to the territory and make desired changes, if any. Representatives may discuss their plans and negotiate with other representatives during this round.

Round 4 (Ten minutes): Teams will reconvene to discuss results. Representatives may receive coaching and instructions from other team members at this time.

Round 5 (Ten minutes): All team members will accompany their representatives to the territory and observe as their representative negotiates for them with the other groups' representatives. Desired changes will be made by team representatives. Only the representatives may negotiate or make adjustments to the team boundaries.

Round 6 (Fifteen minutes): Teams will reconvene in their team meeting areas to discuss their final strategies. Representatives will return to the territory for the final negotiation and/or to make final adjustments to their team's boundaries. Time will be called at the end of this round, and a winning team will be declared by the facilitator.

315. GIVING AND RECEIVING FEEDBACK: CONTRACTING FOR NEW BEHAVIOR

Goals

I. To provide an opportunity for members of a personal-growth group to give and receive feedback on their in-group behavior.

II. To enable participants to set behavioral goals for the remainder of the group experience.

Group Size

Eight to twelve members of an ongoing personal-growth group.

Time Required

Approximately three hours.

Materials

I. A copy of the Giving and Receiving Feedback Work Sheet for each participant.

II. A pencil for each participant.

III. Newsprint and a felt-tipped marker.

Physical Setting

A room with a hard floor or other flat surfaces to facilitate writing tasks.

Process

I. The facilitator explains the goals of the activity and distributes a copy of the Giving and Receiving Feedback Work Sheet and a pencil to each participant. (Two to three minutes.)

II. The facilitator announces that each individual participant is to make a roster of the group, rank ordered according to one dimension that is personally meaningful, e.g., liking, similarity, comfort, power in the group, growth so far. In a separate column beside each name, participants are to write characteristics of each member as they have been exhibited in the group so far and their *reactions* to these behaviors. (Twenty minutes.)

III. Each person is then directed to write *predictions* of what his or her feedback will be. (Ten minutes.)

IV. The participants take turns publishing their data. Recipients of feedback record data relating to them in the last spaces on their work sheets. (Thirty minutes.)

V. After all members have completed giving feedback, they are instructed to consider the feedback that they have given, focusing on the perceptual biases in it. The facilitator then leads a discussion of these biases. (Twenty minutes.)

VI. The participants are instructed to analyze the differences between their actual and their predicted feedback. (Thirty minutes.)

VII. The facilitator focuses on each member in turn, discussing feedback gaps, trends, reactions (surprises, affirmations, puzzlements, etc.). Each individual is then asked to move out of the group while the rest write a prescription for his or her participation during the remainder of the group's life. The individual returns and negotiates planned new behavior and support for experimentation. (One hour.)

VIII. A practice session using the new behavior is held. Each member announces what he or she is going to do in the group and contracts with the other group members for their help in this effort. (Thirty minutes.)

Variations

I. Feedback can be limited to adjectives, critical incidents, one trait, etc.

II. For step II, the participants can write the names of group members along a continuum.

III. Instead of writing in names, each person can physically arrange the group members on a continuum.

IV. Instead of group prescriptions, pairs can be formed to contract for new behavior.

V. Headbands can be used for the practice sessions, with the planned new behaviors written on them.

Similar Structured Experiences: *Vol. I:* Structured Experiences **13**, **17**; *Vol. III:* **57**, **58**; *Vol. IV:* **109**; *'75 Annual:* **146**; *Vol. V:* **170**; *Vol. VI:* **209**.

Suggested Instruments: *Vol. III:* "Feedback Rating Scales," "Group-Behavior Questionnaire"; *'72 Annual:* "Interpersonal Relationship Rating Scale"; *'73 Annual:* "Johari Window Self-Rating Sheet"; *'74 Annual:* "Reactions to Group Situations Test"; *'76 Annual:* "Organization Behavior Describer Survey"; *'77 Annual:* "Interpersonal Check List (ICL)"; *'80 Annual:* "Role Efficacy Scale."

Lecturette Sources: '73 *Annual:* "The Johari Window: A Model for Soliciting and Giving Feedback," "Confrontation: Types, Conditions, and Outcomes"; '74 *Annual:* "The Interpersonal Contract"; '76 *Annual:* "The Awareness Wheel," "Interpersonal Feedback as Consensual Validation of Constructs"; '78 *Annual:* "Contracting: A Process and a Tool"; '79 *Annual:* "Encouraging Others to Change Their Behavior," "Transactions in the Change Process"; '80 *Annual:* "Interaction Process Analysis," "Dimensions of Role Efficacy."

Notes on the Use of "Giving and Receiving Feedback":

Submitted by John E. Jones.

GIVING AND RECEIVING FEEDBACK WORK SHEET

Instructions: Select a dimension on which you believe that members of this group are different, for example, how much you like them, how similar they are to you, how comfortable you are with them, how influential they are in the group, how much they have grown so far, etc. *Write the name of your chosen dimension here.*

Next, rank order all the members of the group (including yourself) on this dimension. Put the "highs" at the top and the "lows" at the bottom. To the right of each name, write adjectives that describe that person's behavior in the group so far and your reactions to that behavior.

Group members in rank order	How I have seen this person in the group so far.
1.	
2.	
3.	
4.	
5.	
6.	
7.	
8.	
9.	
10.	
11.	
12.	

Next, write your predictions of what each person will say about you.

Group member	How I predict this person will see me in the group
1.	
2.	
3.	
4.	
5.	
6.	
7.	
8.	
9.	
10.	
11.	
12.	

Finally, as group members publish their lists, write down how each member ranked you, the dimension, and how that member saw you in the group.

Group member	Dimension	Ranking	How this person has seen me in the group so far
1.			
2.			
3.			
4.			
5.			
6.			
7.			
8.			
9.			
10.			
11.			
12.			

316. GROUP SOCIOGRAM: INTRAGROUP COMMUNICATION

Goals

I. To identify existing patterns of interaction and influence in an intact group.

II. To increase awareness of the effects of group dynamics on intragroup communication patterns.

Group Size

All members of a small intact group, or subgroups of five to seven members each.

Time Required

Approximately one and one-half hours.

Materials

I. A blank 3″ x 5″ index card for each participant.

II. One Tinkertoy® spool for each participant.

III. A set of Tinkertoy rods (two 1″ orange, one 2″ yellow, one 3″ blue, one 5″ red, and one 7″ green) for each participant.

IV. A prepared newsprint "target" with circles of 3″, 6″, and 9″ radii (see diagram) for each group.

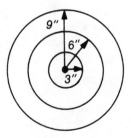

V. Newsprint and a felt-tipped marker.

Physical Setting

A room large enough for each group to work separately with minimum interference from other groups, and a table and chairs for each group.

Process

I. The facilitator introduces the activity and divides the participants into their usual work teams or small groups of five to seven members each. He directs each member to be seated around the group's table and gives each member a blank 3″ x 5″ index card and a Tinkertoy spool into which two short (1″ orange) rods are inserted—one vertically in the center and one horizontally in the side. (Five minutes.)

II. The facilitator directs the members to fold the index cards in half, write their names on the folded cards, and insert them into the slits in the upper ends of their vertical rods (see diagram). The facilitator then places a prepared newsprint "target" in the center of each group's table and puts a marker (any object) in the center of each target. (Five minutes.)

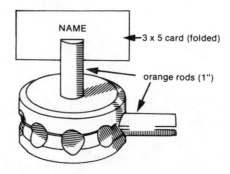

III. The facilitator explains that members will create a symbolic "picture" of their group. He designates the marker as the center or nucleus of the group, symbolizing its goals and purposes. He then directs each member to place his or her spool along or between the circles (i.e., nearer or farther from the center) to signify how closely the member's own goals and interests match the goals and interests of the group. This is to be done nonverbally. (Five minutes.)

IV. The facilitator instructs the group members to discuss the spool placements, without making any changes, for approximately five minutes. At the end of this time, group members are allowed a few minutes to change their own spool markers if desired (they are not permitted to change others). (Ten minutes.)

V. The facilitator provides each member with four additional Tinkertoy rods (yellow, blue, red, and green). He informs the members that the lengths of these rods correspond to the amount of influence or control a person may have in the group; i.e., the longer the rod, the more influence. The facilitator then informs them that the shortest (orange) *vertical* rod presently in the center of each spool represents zero influence, and that they are to replace it (without changing the position of the spool) with one of the new rods. The height of each member's chosen rod will represent the amount of influence or control that that person believes he or she has in the group at the present time. This is to be done nonverbally. (Three minutes.)

VI. The group members are directed to discuss their symbolic decisions without making any changes. After all members have shared their thinking, individuals are permitted to make changes in their own rods or to request another member to make changes. The person asked may comply with or refuse the request. (Ten minutes.)

VII. The facilitator then explains that the short (orange) *horizontal* rod represents the direction in which members are facing. Members are now instructed to move their markers around the target circles closer to those members for whom they feel the greatest closeness (or with whom they have the best communication) and farther away from those for whom they feel the most interpersonal distance (or poorest communication). Members also are directed to face their markers toward or away from other members to indicate positive or negative attraction. This is to be done nonverbally. (Three minutes.)

VIII. The facilitator directs the group members to discuss their placements, without making any changes, for approximately five minutes. Members may then make changes in their relative positions or request other members to make changes. The person asked may comply with or refuse the request. (Ten minutes.)

IX. The facilitator then instructs the group members to discuss the experience, focusing on the reactions members have to the perceptions of others. (Fifteen minutes.)

X. Group members are instructed to discuss the implications of the data generated for the present state of the group's development by focusing on patterns of interaction and sources of influence within the group. (Fifteen minutes.)

XI. The facilitator instructs the group members to discuss applications of the learnings to improve patterns of interaction within the group. (Fifteen minutes.)

Variations

I. Following step VIII, the facilitator can provide additional spools representing absent members and/or other significant individuals. The group members are then encouraged to place these markers in accordance with either how they believe these members would have placed them *or* how they perceive these other individuals in terms of interaction and influence.

II. In the event that there are two or more groups that meet separately but on a common task, time can be set aside following steps IV, VI, and VIII to examine other groups' models. No changes may be made in the other groups' models, and all discussion or questioning except for clarification is postponed until step VIII has been completed. Step IX then includes a comparison between the different ways in which different groups structure themselves to achieve a common goal.

III. Groups can repeat this activity at intervals in their development and keep a graphic record for later comparisons.

Similar Structured Experiences: *Vol. I:* Structured Experience **10**; *Vol. III:* **55**; '72 *Annual:* **79**; '73 *Annual:* **92**; *Vol. VII:* **254**.

Suggested Instruments: *Vol. III:* "Group-Climate Inventory," "Group-Behavior Questionnaire"; '74 *Annual:* "Reactions to Group Situations Test."

Lecturette Sources: '73 *Annual:* "A Model of Group Development"; '74 *Annual:* "Cog's Ladder: A Model of Group Development"; '76 *Annual:* "Role Functions in a Group"; '80 *Annual:* "Interaction Process Analysis."

Notes on the Use of "Group Sociogram":

Submitted by Thomas J. Mallinson, Alan Tolliday, and Ron Sept.

CONTRIBUTORS

William J. Bailey, Ed.D.
Associate Professor
Educational Leadership
College of Education
University of Delaware
Room 206, Willard Hall
Newark, Delaware 19711
(302) 738-1165

Meeky Blizzard
Training Consultant
Rt. 1, Box 916
Beaverton, Oregon 97007
(503) 628-2652

Hyler Bracey, Ph.D.
President
The Atlanta Consulting Group, Inc.
2028 Powers Ferry Road, Suite 190
Atlanta, Georgia 30339
(404) 952-0898

Anne J. Burr
Steelcase, Inc.
1120 36th Street S.E.
Grand Rapids, Michigan 49508
(616) 247-2710

T. F. Carney, Ph.D.
Professor
Organizational Communications
Department of Communication Studies
University of Windsor
Windsor, Province of Ontario
Canada N9B 3P4
(519) 253-4232

Eduardo Casais
Manager, Management and
   Professional Training
SODECO-SAIA S. A.
Grand-Pré 70
Geneva, Switzerland 1202
(Switzerland) (022) 33-55-00

Cynthia Cherrey
Organizational Development Director
North Texas State University Union
NT Station Box 13705
Denton, Texas 76203
(817) 788-2611

Phyliss Cooke, Ph.D.
Director of Professional Services
Dean, Master of Human Resource
   Development Program
University Associates, Inc.
8517 Production Avenue
P. O. Box 26240
San Diego, California 92126
(714) 578-5900

L. B. Day
President
Day-Henry Associates, Inc.
5109 S. W. Oleson Road
Portland, Oregon 97225
(503) 226-4190

Andy F. Farquharson, Ed.D.
Associate Professor and
   Coordinator of Social Work Extension
School of Social Work
University of Victoria
P. O. Box 1700
Victoria, British Columbia, Canada V8W 2Y2
(604) 477-6911

Barbara L. Fisher, Ph.D.
Assistant Professor
Marriage and Family Therapy
Purdue University
109 Child Development and Family Studies
West Lafayette, Indiana 47907
(317) 493-0512

Deborah C. L. Griffith
27 Crosby Road
Chestnut Hill, Massachusetts 02167
(617) 332-3017

Kenneth W. Howard
Prevention and Training Specialist
Chesapeake Substance Abuse Program
2700 Border Road
Chesapeake, Virginia 23325
(804) 543-6847

Stephen C. Iman, Ph.D.
Professor of Management
School of Business
California State Polytechnic University
Pomona, California 91768
(714) 598-4205

John E. Jones, Ph.D.
Senior Vice President
  Research and Development
University Associates, Inc.
8517 Production Avenue
P. O. Box 26240
San Diego, California 92126
(714) 578-5900

H. B. Karp, Ph.D.
Associate Professor
Department of Management
Old Dominion University
Consultant/Owner
Personal Growth Systems
1441 Magnolia Avenue
Norfolk, Virginia 23508
(804) 489-2586

David B. Lyon
262 Blue Ridge Drive
Manchester, Connecticut 06040
(203) 646-0798

Thomas J. Mallinson, Ph.D.
Professor
Department of Communication
Simon Fraser University
Burnaby, British Columbia, Canada V5A 1S6
(604) 291-4381

Don Martin
Counselor Education
North Texas State University
NT Station Box 13487
Denton, Texas 76203
(817) 788-2741

Thomas J. Mason
Instructor of Business Management
Management Team
Brookdale Community College
765 Newman Springs Road
Lincroft, New Jersey 07738
(201) 842-1900

Bernard Nisenholz, Ed.D.
Assistant Professor
Educational Psychology
California State University, Northridge
18111 Nordhoff Street
Northridge, California 91130
(213) 885-3833

Gertrude E. Philpot
Programer
Northeast Utilities
P. O. Box 270
Hartford, Connecticut 06101
(203) 249-5711

Gary N. Powell, Ph.D.
Assistant Professor
Department of Management
  and Administrative Sciences
University of Connecticut
Storrs, Connecticut 06268
(203) 486-3862

Albert A. Ramos, Ph.D.
Manager, Ground Systems Department
Defense and Space Systems Group
TRW, Inc.
P. O. Box 1310
San Bernardino, California 92402
(714) 382-5585

Anthony J. Reilly, Ph.D.
Senior Consultant
University Associates, Inc.
8517 Production Avenue
P. O. Box 26240
San Diego, California 92126
(714) 578-5900

Martin B. Ross, Dr.P.H.
Assistant Professor
  and Associate Director
Program in Health Services Management
School of Public Health
University of California, Los Angeles
Partner, Pointer-Ross and Associates
905 Hilgard Avenue
Los Angeles, California 90024
(213) 825-5773

Roberta G. Sachs, Ph.D.
19 South LaSalle Street, Suite 1100
Chicago, Illinois 60603
(312) 332-4227

Allen J. Schuh, Ph.D.
Professor of Management Sciences
Department of Management Sciences
School of Business and Economics
California State University, Hayward
Hayward, California 94542
(415) 881-3322

Dorianne L. Sehring
37 Debora Drive
Plainview, New York 11803
(516) 938-5638

Ron Sept
Department of Communication
Simon Fraser University
Burnaby, British Columbia, Canada V5A 1S6

Anthony C. Stein
Staff Engineer, Psychologist
Systems Technology, Inc.
13766 South Hawthorne Boulevard
Hawthorne, California 90250
(213) 679-2281

Rich Strand
Department of Psychology
Michigan State University
Snyder Hall
East Lansing, Michigan 48824
(517) 353-4591

Gilles L. Talbot
Professor of Psychology
Social Science Division
St. Lawrence Campus
Champlain Regional College
790 Nérée Tremblay Street
Ste-Foy, Province of Québec
Canada G6V 7G5
(418) 656-6921

Alan Tolliday
Department of Communication
Simon Fraser University
Burnaby, British Columbia, Canada V5A 1S6

Roy Trueblood, Ph.D.
Vice President
The Atlanta Consulting Group, Inc.
2028 Powers Ferry Road, Suite 190
Atlanta, Georgia 30339
(404) 952-0898

Frederic R. Wickert, Ph.D.
Professor of Psychology and
   Graduate Business Administration
Department of Psychology
Michigan State University
Snyder Hall
East Lansing, Michigan 48824
(517) 355-1775

Graham L. Williams
Senior Lecturer
   in Education Management
Department of Education Management
Sheffield City Polytechnic
36 Collegiate Crescent
Sheffield S10 2BP England
(England) 0742-665274

Spencer H. Wyant, Ph.D.
Senior Consultant
Consulting Exchange
P. O. Box 10324
Eugene, Oregon 97440
(503) 485-4471

STRUCTURED EXPERIENCE CATEGORIES